CW00662603

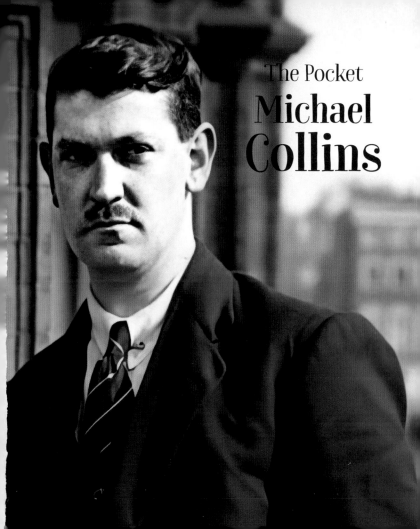

The Pocket
Michael
Collins

Gill Books
Hume Avenue, Park West, Dublin 12

www.gillbooks.ie

Gill Books is an imprint of M.H. Gill & Co.

Copyright © Teapot Press Ltd 2022

ISBN: 978-0-7171-9125-3

This book was created and produced by Teapot Press Ltd

Written by Richard Killeen
Edited by Fiona Biggs
Designed by Tony Potter

Printed in Europe

This book is typeset in Garamond & Dax

A CIP catalogue record for this book is available
from the British Library.

5 4 3 2 1

The Pocket
Michael
Collins
Life, Death & Legacy

Richard Killeen

Gill Books

Contents

CHAPTER 1
Youth

'One day he'll
be a great
man. He'll do
great work for
Ireland.'
Michael Collins Senior

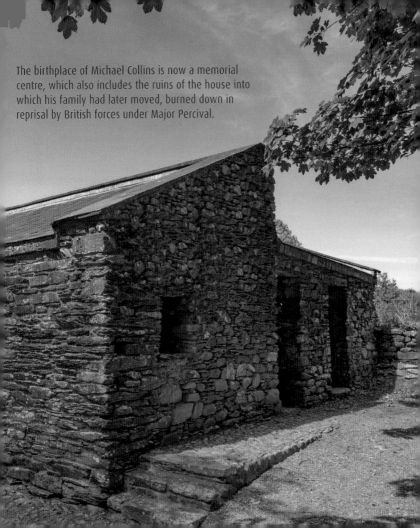

The birthplace of Michael Collins is now a memorial centre, which also includes the ruins of the house into which his family had later moved, burned down in reprisal by British forces under Major Percival.

The Collins family – Ó Coileáin in Irish, which would have been their vernacular until the first half of the 19th century and the language in which both of Michael Collins's parents were fluent, being bilingual – was long established in Munster. The branch of the family with which we are concerned was settled in West Cork, near the market town of Clonakilty. They occupied a tenant farm at a townland called Sam's Cross, just a short way to the north of the road that ran west from Clonakilty to Rosscarbery. Further to the west again, beyond Rosscarbery, lay the town of Skibbereen.

This was a part of Ireland in which there occurred some of the worst horrors of the Great Famine (1845–52), or at least the worst reported horrors. During those years of catastrophe, the population of Ireland, almost 8.2 million in 1841, had been reduced to 6.5 million 10 years later. There followed, in the succeeding decades up to the First World War and beyond, a vast outflow of emigrants abandoning the ruined land and seeking a living of any sort in more prosperous and promising climes. In 1911, the last British census in Ireland showed a population of 4.39 million. Ireland's population had effectively been halved in a single lifetime. Even in Ulster, whose north-eastern corner experienced the Industrial Revolution and the population growth to match it, the overall

A scene outside the gates of a workhouse during the Great Famine.

population decline in the period 1841–1911 was 34 per cent, less drastic than in the island overall, but still demoralising.

West Cork featured heavily in the contemporary reporting of the Famine. In this, perhaps the most potent journal was the *Illustrated London News*, whose images of impoverished cottiers and peasants dying of starvation and related diseases such as relapsing fever brought a shock to the ample breakfast tables of the English middle class. The images are horrific and they come disproportionally from the countryside into which Michael Collins would be born a generation later. Skibbereen, about 30 kilometres west of Clonakilty, was the source of some of the most graphic and disturbing images that were published in the *Illustrated London News*. Clonakilty itself, much nearer to Sam's Cross, also featured in these reports.

Woman begging at Clonakilty.

The Famine left a shadow on Ireland that never went away. In the second half of the 19th century it helped to cultivate a hatred of England and of English rule in Ireland that radicalised Irish nationalism. Up to this point the nationalist demand was for a repeal of the union of 1801, which had created the United Kingdom of Great Britain and Ireland, and a restoration of a devolved Irish parliament to deal with internal affairs. In this endeavour – which did not succeed – Daniel O'Connell (1775–1847) had been the dominant figure. Even towards the end of his life, O'Connell had faced internal opposition from a cultural nationalist ginger group called Young Ireland, some of whom toyed with ideas of republican separatism. O'Connell died in the middle of the Famine. Some Young Irelanders set off a farcical 'rebellion' in County Tipperary in 1848, which was in truth little more than an affray between about 100 insurgents, two of whom were killed and some others injured, and a force of about 45 policemen.

Daniel O'Connell.

After the Famine, the bitterness that it had engendered, especially among those sufficiently resourceful to have got away to America, translated into outright republican separatism. Likewise, old '48 men who had been to France and had absorbed that country's formidable tradition of revolutionary republicanism sought to re-import it to Ireland. It required the energies of these men to effect this radicalisation, for the ordinary surviving Irish back home were prone and exhausted after the deluge.

These twin forces met in 1858. In February of that year, a group in New York constituted themselves as 'the Irish Revolutionary Committee' and appointed James Stephens as head of the movement. Stephens, a civil engineer by profession and a man of restless energy and intelligence, had been injured in the 1848 affray; he was prominent among those who had been to Paris where he got to know leading republican figures – many of them Italian exiles – as well as other Irish exiles of a temper similar to his own. Back in Ireland, Stephens formally established the Irish Revolutionary Brotherhood (later to become the Irish Republican Brotherhood, or IRB) on St Patrick's Day, 17 March 1858. The following year, John O'Mahony founded the Fenian Brotherhood in New York in April 1859. It was a twin of the IRB and gave the entire Irish republican separatist tradition its generic name, the Fenians.

James Stephens, Fenian.

This republican sensibility was not absent in West Cork. In May 1858, Jeremiah O'Donovan founded the Phoenix National and Literary Society in Skibbereen. O'Donovan was from Rosscarbery, about halfway between Clonakilty and Skibbereen, and styled himself accordingly. He is known to history as Jeremiah O'Donovan Rossa, and he bequeathed a new boys' name to Ireland. His new society was soon folded into the IRB. As for Rossa himself, he became business manager of Stephens's paper, the *Irish People*, in the mid-1860s, and was arrested and sentenced to 20 years' penal servitude for sedition. He was treated cruelly in prison but was released in 1871 on condition that he did not return to Ireland. He went to the United States.

While there, Rossa edited a republican newspaper and published a book of prison memoirs and a number of other titles. He was also a prime mover in the dynamite bomb campaign in Britain in the 1880s, funded from the United States, which anticipated the tactics of the IRA a century later. Afterwards, his influence declined; he died in 1915, aged 84, at Staten Island, New York. His body was repatriated to Ireland and buried in Glasnevin Cemetery after a full-dress Fenian funeral. Patrick Pearse's eulogy over his body is one of the greatest pieces of oratory in Irish history.

1 August 1915, funeral procession of Fenian Jeremiah O'Donovan Rossa. Trams drew to a halt and crowds lined the streets as the coffin passed.

In the 1880s, while Rossa's 'skirmishers' were letting off bombs in London, Ireland was in the throes of the Land War. A collapse in agricultural prices in the late 1870s – prompted by the opening up of the huge fertile plains of Argentina and the United States, together with the development of fast, refrigerated shipping – prompted a rural crisis throughout Europe, which could not match the New World's astonishing economies of scale. The people most at risk from this development were the tenant farmers who had survived the Famine 30 years earlier and were determined that no such calamity would ever be visited on them again.

The Land War fell into two parts, the first from 1879 to 1882 and the second – known as the Plan of Campaign – in the last few years of the 1880s. It wasn't pretty and there was a high level of agrarian crime, damage to property and livestock, and boycotting (the word was coined during the agitation). Likewise, there was a robust push-back from the British authorities, especially during the Plan of Campaign. Overall, however, it represented the ruin of the landed class, from which any legitimacy was fast flowing away. Several Land Acts were passed in London to give the tenants rights that compromised the strict principles of English property law; it was a case of terrible necessity and an acknowledgment of Irish difference.

The heart and soul of these land agitations were tenant farmers like the Collins family of Sam's Cross. This was the world into which Michael Collins was born on 16 October 1890.

He was the youngest of eight. There were two brothers and five sisters before him. At the time of his birth, his father, Michael John Collins, was 75 years of age. He had married late, at the age

Members of the RIC evict T. Birmingham from his house in Moyasta on the Vandeleur Estate in County Clare, July 1888, during the Plan of Campaign.

of 60. His wife was Mary Anne O'Brien, also from the locality. She was 23 when she married Collins. She bore Michael senior a child every other year for the first 15 years of their marriage. They lived in a house called Woodfield, at Sam's Cross.

Michael Collins senior was of that class of reasonably substantial tenant farmers that had recovered from the Famine and was the principal beneficiary of the Land Acts. These pieces of legislation would culminate in the Wyndham Act of 1903, whereby the Conservative government of the day bought out the landlord interest in the old estates (leaving only demesne lands where requested) and transferred title to the former tenants, financing these purchases by government loans backed by long-term Treasury bonds.

Michael Collins senior did not live to benefit from these transactions. He died, aged 81, in 1896, leaving his widow and older sons to continue farming their 90-acre tenancy. He had been a man of substance and education, having a knowledge of the classics and of mathematics. This was not at all the conventional caricature of the Irish tenant farmer – a caricature made in England for domestic consumption – but equally does not seem to have been entirely typical of the tenant farmer class. Michael senior had been noted in his day as a somewhat exceptional person.

None the less, he can't have been that exceptional. Without people like him, with some education – perhaps more than history has given them credit for – and the independence of mind and spirit that comes with it, it is hard to see how a movement such as the Land League could have mobilised so effectively – its criminal undertow notwithstanding – or how its political cousin, the Home Rule movement, could have proved so effective. Of course, Home Rule had the genius of Parnell to guide it, but when it came to the fatal split in 1890 – just a few weeks after Michael Collins was born – more than one historian has noted that it was the more independent-minded and accomplished members of the Irish Party that abandoned Parnell. Not least among them was the waspishly brilliant Timothy Healy, another

Timothy Healy, as portrayed in *Vanity Fair*.

'He comes from a brainy Cork family.'

The young Michael Collins.

West Cork man, a barrister and journalist of considerable ability, and one destined to outlive the newborn child in Woodfield.

From the first, Michael – the youngest – was adored by his siblings. It was soon evident that he was a bright and intelligent child, quick on the uptake. He read and computed early and easily and from a young age showed an urge to be the leader in most things, even in innocent games with other children. Thus was the boy father to the man, for in the years of his pomp he simply believed that he could do everything better than everyone else, and he was usually right.

His formal education began locally in the national school at Lisavaird in Rosscarbery before continuing at the national school in Clonakilty. At Lisavaird, the teacher was one Denis Lyons, an IRB man, a disciplinarian who inculcated a strongly nationalist and republican reading of Irish history in his charges. Lyons was merely echoing what little Michael Collins had heard at home. His father was an ardent nationalist; he seems to have been in the IRB, and he certainly carried within him the tradition of dispossession so common among his class and creed all across Ireland. The rule of the landlord class was illegitimate, in this reading, for their property rested on the expropriation of what had properly belonged to others – our ancestors – from whom it had been stolen. This sensibility was a commonplace among the Catholic Irish generally, but especially strong among those, like the Collins clan, who felt that, had history been kinder to them, it would have been they who would have been lords of the land.

All this was cross-pollinated with the toxin of religion. Nearly every foreign traveller in Ireland in the 19th century remarked on the extraordinarily close bond of affection and loyalty that existed between priests and people. As early as Daniel O'Connell's time, 60 years before Michael Collins was born, this was remarked on by travellers as diverse as Alexis de Tocqueville and William Makepeace Thackeray. After the disaster of the Famine, the Catholic Church was the one old institution still standing that commanded social leadership and prestige, a process that lasted deep into the 20th century before it finally curdled.

The 19th century was an age of religious controversy. Sectarian rivalries and hatred were not confined to provinces such as Ulster. A significant part of the indifferent British response to the Irish Famine had been to view the Irish peasants as heretic papists who needed the providential wrath of the Protestant God (resident in Charing Cross) to sort them out. In Ireland, theological and agrarian hatreds were horribly tangled.

All this was a heady brew for the mind of what was very obviously an exceptionally bright boy. Collins read Shakespeare and George Eliot and excelled at school. So there was a tussle between inherited resentments on the one hand and the glories of English literature on the other. There is no evidence of the Collins family having any special animus towards Protestants; indeed, in West Cork – given a larger-than-usual Protestant minority – inter-faith relations appear to have been relaxed and accommodating.

Young Collins did not confine his reading to the English canon. From an early age, he was immersed in Irish nationalist literature as well. As he entered his teens, he also devoured the journalism of advanced nationalism, not least that of Arthur Griffith's *United Irishman*. When Michael was six his father died, but his legacy of militant nationalism and uncompromising

Arthur Griffith addresses a crowd in July 1922.

Arthur Griffith, founding leader of Sinn Féin and later President of Dáil Éireann, who died in August 1922.

opposition to landlordism lived on in his youngest son.

One of the effects of the Wyndham Act of 1903 was to remove the land question from the mainstream political agenda, but in so doing it threw the spotlight afresh on the constitutional status of Ireland. In 1900, when Collins was 10, the Irish Party was reunited following the trauma of the Parnell split. But alongside this development, there arose a series of ginger groups of more advanced nationalists, for whom Home Rule was not enough. These ranged from the Fenians – who were low in the water at this time but headed for a spectacular resurrection – to Arthur Griffith's new grouping, Sinn Féin, founded in 1905. These more advanced nationalists had organised the celebrations to commemorate the centenary of the 1798 rising; they had led the opposition to Queen Victoria's visit to Ireland in 1900;

and they positioned themselves generally to the left of the Irish Parliamentary Party (IPP).

It was to this segment of Irish nationalism that young Michael Collins was drawn. There is little doubt that his father would have approved. His teacher, Denis Lyons, the old IRB man, certainly did. These twin influences steered him towards this more robust iteration of the nationalist demand, but influence can only carry a person so far, and Collins also showed an independence of thought and spirit from an early age. His militancy was an expression of his personality. He was ardent, athletic, hot-tempered and domineering, looking to take the lead in most things, a quality that remained with him all his short life. It accounted both for the leadership role he was to play in the final fight for independence and also for the hostility that he attracted from some colleagues who felt bruised by his belligerent behaviour.

Years later, Collins summarised his foundational views:

'It was not only by British armed occupation that Ireland was subdued. It was also by means of the destruction, after great effort, of our Gaelic civilisation. This destruction brought upon us the loss almost of nationality itself. For the last hundred years or more Ireland has been a nation in little more than name.

'Britain wanted us for her own economic ends, as well as to satisfy her love of conquest. It was found, however, that Ireland was not an easy country to conquer, nor to use for the purposes for which conquests were made. We had a native culture. We had a social system of our own. We had an economic organisation. We had a code of laws which fitted us.'

This was standard IRB/Fenian analysis, which Collins imbibed early from his father and from Denis Lyons. There was one other very important influence on the young Michael Collins, one that affected his entire generation. The cultural revival of the 1890s had seen the astonishing success of the Gaelic League and the movement to revive the Irish language. Collins was an enthusiast for the language from an early age. While most of his surviving correspondence is in English, his salutations and signature were often in Irish: thus, a chara/friend, the standard salutation, while signing off as Micheál Ó Coileáin. Even after he moved to London to work in a post office at the age of 15, he continued his deep involvement with the language movement.

Likewise, he was a Gaelic games enthusiast. He was developing into a splendid athlete and was drawn from an early age to the Gaelic Athletic Association. This had been founded in 1884 and

had survived a series of near-death crises in the 1890s, but had pulled through to grow into one of the central pillars of Irish nationalism in the 20th century, the largest Irish sporting organisation and (it is claimed) the largest amateur sports body in the world. Its primary remit was to revive the ancient sport of hurling, which it did. But it also developed a football code that was distinct from both soccer and rugby; Gaelic football is still the most popular sport in Ireland. Michael Collins played both hurling and football, at first in West Cork and later in London. Critically, the GAA was from the very start dominated by the Fenians. Although out of

Michael Cusack, Irish teacher and founder of the Gaelic Athletic Association.

obvious political favour for many years, the Fenians had control of this great populist and popular organisation, through which they could keep their influence renewed.

In 1905, Collins finished his formal schooling. He went to Clonakilty to live with P. J. O'Driscoll, the proprietor of a small local newspaper who was married to Collins's sister Margaret. His principal purpose was to study for the post office entrance examination but inevitably, with his quick intelligence and wit, he began to acquire the rudiments of journalism. He learned to type and wrote some short pieces for the paper. Moreover, he saw for the first time the financial operations of a commercial enterprise, albeit a very modest one, discovering a talent for numbers that would bring him some spectacular achievements later on.

He spent over a year with the O'Driscolls in Clonakilty before sitting the examination, which he passed. He was offered a job in the Post Office Savings Bank in West Kensington in London. Not yet 16, he moved to the English capital to take up the job. He was to spend the next nine years there, lodging with his sister Hannie in the same area. She too worked in the post office. Michael Collins was out in the world.

A view of the main block of Blythe House, West Kensington, London, where Michael Collins worked. From a commemorative album, 1924.

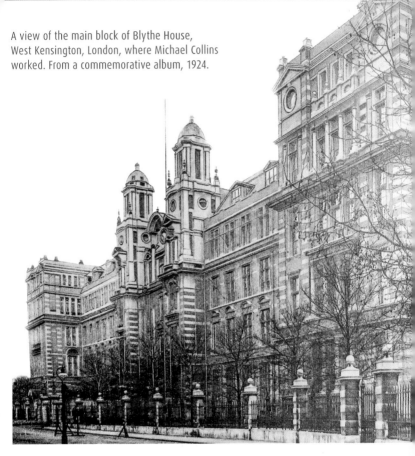

CHAPTER 2
The London Years

'Give us the
future … we've
had enough of
your past …
give us back our
country to live in
– to grow in …
to love.'

Michael Collins

In his London years, Collins worked for four different employers. He started with the Post Office Savings Bank, working as a clerk. In 1910, he moved to the city to work for the stockbroking firm of Horne & Co., for whom he acted as a junior manager supervising the various messengers that the company deployed around London. He then went to work as a clerk for the Board of Trade, having studied at night in King's College and having taken the civil service entry examination. But when the First World War broke out in August 1914, the danger of conscription arose. In fact, it did not become a live issue until the passing of the Military Service Act of 1916, the United Kingdom choosing to fight the first half of the war with a volunteer army. But that was not obvious in 1914 and the potential danger of being called up brought pressure from the family back in Ireland to move to Chicago, where his elder brother Pat was already established. Instead, Collins found a halfway house in London, by moving to the local office of the Guaranty Trust Co. of New York.

All this was not exactly approaching the summit of high finance, but it did deepen Collins's understanding of financial matters, for which he had shown an early aptitude in O'Driscoll's in Clonakilty. He later wrote that 'the trade I know best is the financial trade, but from study and observation I have acquired

Jacques-Emile Blanche, *Ludgate Circus: Entrance to the City*, 1910.

a wide knowledge of social and economic conditions and have specially studied the building trade and unskilled labour.'

This furious self-improvement, focused on the acquisition of financial knowledge, has led Tim Pat Coogan, Collins's most authoritative modern biographer, to suggest that Collins could easily have become a wealthy man had he chosen to pursue a financial career, for which he demonstrated such obvious aptitude. But temperamentally he had no interest in such a course.

However, no time is ever totally wasted. The money gene in Collins, which he cultivated so assiduously in London, would in due course come to play an indispensable role in the final days of the fight for Irish freedom. In early 1919, he became Minister of Finance in the Dáil administration – a shadow government of insurgents deemed illegal by the British authorities but which commanded a high degree of legitimacy in the eyes of the Irish nationalist population – and promptly oversaw the raising of a Dáil loan of more than £350,000, which helped to finance the work of the shadow government. The entire management of this audacious venture was in Collins's hands at a time when he was also engaged in directing military affairs during the early days of the War of Independence. Not bad for a lad who had left school at

Michael Collins, Minister
of Finance, 1919.

15 and never held a position greater than that of junior bank clerk! This was no ordinary man.

His time in London had been well spent. By study, he had built on that natural facility for finance that had manifested itself so early. On his own evidence, he became familiar with basic accountancy skills: he mastered double-entry bookkeeping and could make trial balances and balance sheets. He also learned the importance of systematic management and of structured organisation, aptitudes that would again stand to him in later years, to the great benefit of the independence movement, if not always to the psychological comfort of less driven colleagues, some of whom came to hate his imperious insistence on efficiency and punctuality. Like many a driven and assertive person Collins was not one to suffer fools gladly: a temperament such as his was bound to make enemies along the way. But the way led to an achievement that would have seemed beyond dreaming when Collins was still in London. The seeds planted there germinated back in Ireland half a decade later.

That was the English world in which Collins moved for nine years in London. It was a world that was external to him. But there was also an internal, personal cultural world which, despite geography and location, was substantially Ireland-focused. The external world of financial acumen was a product of Collins's English experience and could hardly have matured as it did without that experience. But his internal, cultural formation was mostly concentrated on Ireland and Irish cultural interests in the English capital.

'The strength of the nation will be the strength of the spirit of the whole people.'

Michael Collins,
A Path to Freedom

W.B. Yeats

Along with Dublin, London was a centre of Irish cultural revival in the late nineteeth and early twentieth centuries. For example, the Irish Literary Society was founded in London in 1892 by William Butler Yeats, T. W. Rolleston and Charles Gavan Duffy.

35

While Collins was not in Ireland, he was of Ireland – and he had no desire to be of anywhere else. While he continued his immersion in English literature and theatre – for which he developed a genuine enthusiasm – his principal cultural interests were Irish.

He renewed his membership of the GAA by becoming a member of the Geraldines club, for whom he played both football and hurling with his customary belligerence. Significantly, he also became treasurer of the club and in due time would hold the position of treasurer to the entire GAA in London. He also joined – or rejoined – the Gaelic League. His devotion to the Irish language never wavered and was part of his overall commitment to what was called the cause of Irish-Ireland. This was a sentiment that stressed the autonomy of things Irish in Ireland: the Irish language, of course, but also 'advanced' politics rooted in Anglophobia (Collins was, for instance, a keen supporter of the GAA ban on 'foreign', i.e. English, games), support for Irish manufactures and in general a disposition to seek an Irish sensibility on any issue if it were possible to find one.

This echoed the broad policies of Sinn Féin, of which Collins was a member. It also echoed the editorial line of *The Leader*, a very successful and influential Dublin newspaper owned and edited by a journalist of genius, D. P. Moran. Moran was a singular character, tetchy, intolerant and a great detractor. Despite the general closeness of their views, he took against Arthur Griffith; he was shrill in his dislike of the English, but even more so in his contempt for those members of the Irish middle class who aped English ways and manners, calling them shoneens and West Brits. Protestants were 'sour-faces' and were invited to learn their place – below the salt – in the new Ireland ahead.

So, while Moran was prepared to say out loud what other, more temperate or discreet people might think privately, he was on to something. There was a confluence of interests flowing together in the first decade of the 20th century – the GAA, the Gaelic League, Sinn Féin and *The Leader* – all representing a more radical and culturally inflected nationalism than the Irish Parliamentary Party at Westminster was offering. For the moment, the party had the numbers and seemed invincible. But eventually, the hour struck for the radicals.

D. P. Moran.

Gaelic League poster from 1913, contrasting a proud, independent Éire with a craven, dependent West Britain.

Collins was involved, indeed immersed, in this world. His active involvement both as player and administrator in the GAA won him a wide circle of friends within the London-Irish community. Indeed, his membership of the Gaelic League yielded the added bonus of female company – unlike the wholly masculine world of the GAA. Collins was a handsome, athletic young man, just shy of six feet tall, and, unsurprisingly, attractive to girls. A female cousin of his – also a post office worker – declared that all the girls in the Gaelic League were mad about him. This is perhaps a pardonable exaggeration on the part of the cousin, but young women were certainly not indifferent to Michael Collins.

A glimpse into how Collins himself recalls his London years comes in a quote – properly repeated in most work about him – from an exchange he had later in life with P. S. O'Hegarty, a senior figure in the Gaelic League and later a public servant and writer of distinction, to whom he recalled this anecdote:

'Once, years ago, a crowd of us were going along the Shepherd's Bush Road when out of a lane came a chap with a donkey – just the sort of donkey and just the sort of cart they have at home. He came out quite suddenly and abruptly and we all cheered him. Nobody who has not been an exile will understand me, but I stand for that.'

His involvement with Sinn Féin led to a number of invitations to deliver papers on various aspects of Irish social and political life. In one such paper, the young firebrand excoriated the Irish Catholic hierarchy for being insufficiently supportive of the national cause – by which, no doubt, he meant Sinn Féin's branch of advanced nationalism – and suggested that the best way to deal with them was to exterminate them! This was a shocking view for any Irish Catholic of whatever political stripe to express, but it marks an early appearance of that ruthlessness of character and brutality of logic for which he was to become famous within a few short years.

He then took a step beyond Sinn Féin. In late 1909, a fellow post office worker, Sam Maguire – the man for whom the All-Ireland Senior Football trophy is named – inducted Michael Collins into the IRB. The secret ceremony took place in Barnsbury, just north of King's Cross and about halfway between Camden Town and Islington. He was now a Fenian in earnest.

A few years later, in 1912, it seemed as if the IPP had achieved its moment of glory. The Third Home Rule Bill was passed, although its application was delayed by two years – which were, as things turned out, to prove crucial – because of the bill's predictable defeat in the House of Lords. Their lordships' absolute veto had been done away with a few years earlier and a power of delay was the residue left to them. The passage of the Home Rule Act seemed a total vindication for the Irish Party and its leader, John Redmond, who had fulfilled Parnell's dream. Advanced nationalists must have seemed more marginal than ever. But Home Rule had prompted the most violent opposition in Protestant Ulster, which threatened secession rather than be ruled by Roman Catholics. In this, they had the support of Tory ultras in Britain and even of the Tory leadership: the leader of the

John Redmond with his wife and daughter.

Conservative and Unionist Party of Great
Britain and Ireland was Andrew Bonar Law,
born in New Brunswick, Canada, but the
son of a Presbyterian minister originally
from Coleraine, County Derry. So he had
Ulster Protestant blood in his veins and in
his enthusiasm for their cause, he brought the
party of throne and altar to the very edge of
treason.

At the heart of the Ulster resistance
to Home Rule lay the military muscle
of the Ulster Volunteer Force (UVF), a
militia formed under the gaze of the Ulster
leadership, Edward Carson and James Craig,
which brazenly and in defiance of the law
landed a cargo of guns and ammunition –
sourced from a dealer in Hamburg – at the
port of Larne, County Antrim, just north of
Belfast. The presence of the UVF prompted
an equal and opposite reaction among
southern nationalists, who formed their
own militia. In November 1913, the Irish

Sir Edward Carson.

Volunteers were formed, ostensibly to defend Home Rule – although against whom was not stated, because the only body against which it might have so defended Home Rule was the UVF, which would have meant civil war.

At any rate, the Volunteers echoed the UVF by importing arms and ammunition from the continent, although unlike in Ulster where the authorities were complacent and looked the other way during the Larne landing, the Dublin landing was met with a police response that eventually resulted in the deaths of four civilians. The political temperature in Ireland was rising, and that could only stand to benefit the radicals on both sides. Indeed, the IRB had a disproportionate influence on the Irish Volunteers from the very start. Typically, they operated secretively, keeping the formal leaders of the Volunteers in the dark. The head of the Volunteers was a courtly scholar, Eoin Mac Néill, who had also been a founder of the Gaelic League. He was no match for the rough stuff in which the Fenians revelled.

On 25 April 1914, Michael Collins joined the Irish Volunteers, and was sworn in to the No. 1 London Company by his close friend from West Cork, Sean Hurley. So Collins was now part of the IRB element that was manoeuvring secretly within the Irish Volunteers. He was trusted, he was popular in advanced nationalist circles in London and he had impressed most people with whom he had come into contact. Now, however, he was moving towards the very centre of Irish republican radicalism.

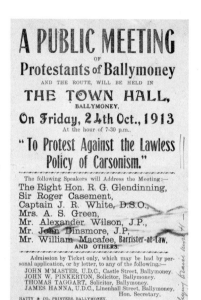

1913 poster advertising a Protestant public meeting in Ballymoney, County Antrim, to protest against Carson's policies.

Eoin Mac Néill.

Collins retained an exceptional intellectual curiosity. In all his years in London, he had been an avid reader both in the Irish nationalist tradition and in the mainstream of English literature. He was familiar with the work of the major figures of late 19th-century English fiction such as Thomas Hardy and Joseph Conrad. He was fortunate in that regard in his timing: the 1890s brought a huge expansion in British publishing, making available popular editions of substantial writers at accessible prices. For an autodidact like Collins, who devoured books, this was a happy conjunction of circumstances.

Collins was first and last a man of action, and men of action are not always cerebral, or intellectually curious, or big readers. Some are, but more are not. Collins was certainly in the former category. His reading not only provided the education he had been unable to pursue formally beyond the age of 15, it also sharpened his whole mental acuity: his was a well-stocked mind. And it was a mind that was almost intuitively given to structure, the organisation of thought and the clarity of intellect that can cut to the heart of a problem. Some big readers withdraw into a private world, as in a university study or common room. Others – Churchill and de Gaulle are headline examples – draw on the riches of their reading to project their personalities into the public sphere. That was part of what gave Michael Collins his extraordinary charisma and authority. Over the next year, he was to think through a series of military problems for the Irish Volunteers that would transform the performance of the organisation and set Ireland on the road to revolution.

Michael Collins as a young recruit.

But first, he had to return to Ireland. He had been in London for nine years, years that had formed him and made him

Thomas Clarke.

what he now was. He gave his notice to the Guaranty Trust Company, telling them that he was intending to 'join up'. They naturally assumed that he meant the British war effort and rewarded him with an extra week's pay upon severance. This he promptly donated to the IRB. He was joining up, all right, for by now he was sufficiently trusted in the counsels of that secretive organisation to have been given the news that a rising was being planned in Ireland while the British were fighting their existential war in Europe: the old Fenian trope of England's difficulty being Ireland's opportunity.

In fact, the degree of trust extended to him was all the more remarkable when one considers that it was not the Irish Volunteers that were planning the rising; Mac Néill and the other leaders were thoroughly in the dark, as was the leadership of the IRB itself. The actual

Patrick Pearse.

plotters were a secret cabal within the IRB that styled itself the Military Council. Its leading figures were Tom Clarke, a veteran Fenian from the 1880s bombing campaign, his acolyte and disciple Seán MacDermott, the teacher and journalist Patrick Pearse and the labour leader and socialist theoretician James Connolly.

So the rising was being planned by a group within a group within a group. It managed to conceal its purpose until the very last moment. Yet months out from the event itself, this ultra-secret group reposed sufficient confidence in the young London-Irishman from West Cork to take him into their counsels. He did not hesitate. Over the fruitless pleas of his sister Hannie, who was sure that it would all end badly, Michael Collins sailed for Dublin. It was 15 January 1916. He had just turned 25 years of age.

Seán MacDermott.

CHAPTER 3
The Easter Rising

'That valiant effort and the martyrdom that followed 1916 finally awoke the sleeping spirit of Ireland.'

Michael Collins

When Collins returned to Dublin, it was to take part in the proposed rising. The fact that knowledge of it had been shared with him was a mark of the trust that was already invested in him. The Military Council – representing the most radical and irreconcilable element in the Fenian tradition – concealed their plans not only from Mac Néill and the formal leadership of the Irish Volunteers, whose name and uniforms they proposed to hijack, but also from the leadership of the IRB itself. The leaders of the rising were understandably neurotic about secrecy, even going so far as to kidnap Bulmer Hobson, a very senior IRB man, on the eve

of the rising, when they feared that he might reveal their plans and scupper the whole thing.

Hobson was a much more senior figure in the Fenian firmament than Michael Collins, very well respected and a formidable personality. So if someone like him was being kept in the dark, it emphasises the degree to which the young man from West Cork now had the trust of the most diehard Fenians.

Collins lodged in the village of Kimmage, to the south of the city, later to become a suburb as the city expanded. He had secured a position with the Plunkett family, whose large house sat on the site of an old

Bulmer Hobson.

mill and was surrounded by a farm of eight acres. His job was basically to keep the family books in order, a task that was never going to consume a great deal of his time. Instead, he became a confidant of one of the family members, Joseph, who was himself a member of the Military Council planning the rising.

By Irish standards, the Plunketts were well-to-do, if not downright rich. The family had originally made its money in building, although they could claim a more ancient lineage that lifted them above trade: they were a cadet branch of one of the ancient Hiberno-Norman families of the Pale, which produced persons as different as St Oliver Plunkett and the Barons Dunsany. Many of the burgeoning Victorian middle-class suburbs on the south side of Dublin had been developed by Joseph's grandfather. Joseph's father, George, born in 1851, was able to live the life of a scholarly gentleman of independent means.

George Plunkett was an enthusiast for the preservation of the Irish language, a senior figure in the Irish National Literary Society and a magazine proprietor and editor. Along the way, he became a papal count for donating money to Catholic causes, and was known ever after as George Noble, Count Plunkett. Later, he was to be the director of the National Museum, a vice-president of the Royal Irish Academy and president of the Royal Society of Antiquaries of Ireland. All in all, a cultural ornament, and a most improbable father of a martyred republican revolutionary.

Joseph Mary Plunkett was born in 1887 and educated privately at elite Jesuit schools: Belvedere in Dublin and Stonyhurst in Lancashire. He was a delicate youth, having contracted tuberculosis. He spent some time in Mediterranean countries in the hope of arresting the advance of the disease, this being a standard practice for those that could afford it. At Stonyhurst, his involvement with the Officer Training Corps gave him a rudimentary insight into military tactics which he later placed at the service of the IRB.

Back in Ireland, he joined the Gaelic League and made the classic transition towards militant republicanism. He joined the IRB in 1915, becoming their principal military strategist. He went to Germany to solicit arms, where he was received with sufficient interest that he got a meeting with the imperial chancellor, Theobald Von Bethmann Hollweg. His efforts resulted in a shipment that was almost landed in County Kerry on the weekend preceding the rising. The famous British cipher room in London had, however, cracked the German codes (including the

Joseph Mary Plunkett.

celebrated Zimmermann Telegram that effectively brought the United States into the First World War on the Allied side). They saw communications between Berlin and the American Fenians – acting as go-betweens for Plunkett and the Military Council – which gave them knowledge of the shipment and its destination. The ship sailed on and was scuttled in Cork harbour.

As a member of the Military Council it was largely Joseph Plunkett's plan of scattered garrisons around the city that was actually carried into effect once the rising began. He himself, although now desperately ill with the tuberculosis that was killing him, fought as best he could with the GPO garrison, with Michael Collins acting as his aide-de-camp.

Contemporary American poster promoting Irish independence.

Collins was not the only guest at Larkfield. Tommy Dillon, Joseph Plunkett's brother-in-law – he was married to Geraldine Plunkett – was there working as a bomb-maker. Also around the place was Rory O'Connor, a qualified and experienced engineer, who helped Dillon in this endeavour. O'Connor thought the world of Collins and said so; tragically, they were both to die young on opposite sides of the Civil War. In these early months of 1916, Larkfield was one of the nerve centres of the plot that would lead to the Easter Rising.

In the few months leading up to the rising, Collins did not neglect his cultural and language interests. Indeed, he

Thomas Dillon, professor of chemistry, and Geraldine Plunkett Dillon, writer and nationalist, in 1940.

endorsed them in the most decisive manner possible by joining the Keating Branch of the Gaelic League. The Keating Branch was named for the 17th-century poet and historian Seathrún Céitinn/Geoffrey Keating, whose most famous work was Foras Feasa ar Éirinn or History of Ireland, the first great narrative history of the country from ancient times until the arrival of the Normans in the 12th century. It was written partly to challenge what Keating saw as a whole tradition of English Hibernophobia, starting with the writings of Giraldus Cambrensis and continuing down to writers like the poet Edmund Spenser. This consistent tradition represented the Irish people as backward and savage; it was Keating's ambition to rescue his people from these slanders. Moreover, Keating was an ardent Catholic who had written in defence of the Mass and was a champion of the Counter-Reformation.

Keating was therefore an early exponent of that junction between faith and fatherland that was to play such a headline part in subsequent Irish history. It is hardly surprising that when a Gaelic League branch was named for him – it was founded in 1901 – it tended to attract nationalist radicals. It had a strong well-educated Munster membership and it soon attracted a reputation for Fenian influence; it was a recruiting ground for both the Irish

Volunteers and the IRB. Its contemporary influence was out of proportion to its numbers, but it suited Collins down to the ground.

All this political and cultural formation came to a head at the Easter weekend of 1916. To his horror, Eoin Mac Néill found out about the plans for a rising at the last minute. He issued a countermanding order, forbidding all Volunteer activity. Its effect was to confine the rising, when it eventually broke out a day late on Easter Monday, largely to Dublin. It also ensured that even in Dublin, the turnout was smaller than intended, with only about 1,200 Volunteers turning up. The ones who did mustered at Liberty Hall on Eden Quay; the various battalions dispersed to their positions and occupied them; and the main garrison force, of which Collins was a part, made for the General Post Office on Sackville (now O'Connell) Street.

Eoin Mac Néill, Chief of Staff of the Irish Volunteers, 1916.

'Whoever controls Dublin controls Ireland.'
Michael Collins

After the Bombardment by Archibald McGoogan. The area destroyed on the eastern side of Sackville Street reached from Cathedral Street to O'Connell Bridge. The only objects standing were the facade of Clery's drapery warehouse, the outer walls of the Hibernian Branch Bank and the shell of the D.B.C. premises.

Telephone box inside the GPO.

Collins's first action in the GPO, once the building had been invested, was to discover two tierces of stout and pour them down a drain (a tierce was a cask containing about 35 gallons or 159 litres; you'd have to wonder what they were doing in a post office). He claimed that alcohol had been the curse of previous rebel efforts but it wasn't going to affect this one. He next turned to one Second Lieutenant A. D. Chalmers of the 14th Royal Fusiliers who had popped into the GPO to send a telegram to his wife in London. He informed Chalmers that he was a prisoner and would be interrogated. So saying, he had him covered by Captain W. J. Brennan-Whitmore from Wexford – who was to have an adventurous Easter week himself in command of a sub-garrison (in fact, no more than a sturdy barricade) across the road at the top of North Earl Street – and went over to one of the telephone booths and yanked out the wire. With this, he trussed the wretched Chalmers before hoisting him on his back and dumping him in the booth.

A policeman, one Constable Dunphy of the Dublin Metropolitan Police, also found himself caught up in this confusion. 'Please don't shoot me,' he cried, 'I've done no harm.' To which Collins replied crisply: 'We don't shoot prisoners.' He then had him taken to an upstairs room and locked in. Collins's principal duties during the rising were in the operations room at the GPO, a somewhat surreal setting since their whole disposition was, in military terms, defensive-passive. Once the British had reacted by Tuesday afternoon and thrown a cordon around the city centre – isolating the GPO from all the other positions except the Four Courts – the rebels had no strategic options at all. The poring over maps and the discussing of speculative and impractical plans helped to sow the first doubts in Collins's practical mind about the thinking behind the entire enterprise.

The rising was an exercise in theatre, in gesture. James Connolly himself, the most practical of the leaders and the one for whom Collins had the greatest admiration, had admitted as much to his trade union colleague William O'Brien when he said to him: 'Bill, we are going out to be slaughtered.' The emotional republican in Collins understood this at one level, but the practical Collins did not feel it in his viscera. The thought formed in his head that gestures may be heroic and poetic but they are no way to win. It was no accident that he was ever after cool in his judgement

Irish Citizen Army members on a training exercise on the roof of Liberty Hall prior to the Easter Rising.

of Pearse, the high priest of poetic gesture, although remaining careful to observe the pieties. Next time, he thought – and there will be a next time – we'll do whatever it takes to win, and to hell with gestures.

None the less, it was the gesture that ultimately captured the Irish nationalist imagination. The Easter Rising is seen as the foundation event that led to the birth of the independent state. It might be fairer to describe it as a transformative event, for Irish nationalism had been on the go for a century or more before the rising, which merely raised the ante quite dramatically. That is a solid historical point but it has little purchase on the public imagination. In that sense, Pearse was right and Collins was wrong. Where Collins was right was in recognising that, in terms of projecting political and military ambition, the rising had been a dead end. It was little more than a reprise of the various 1848 affrays across Europe or the Paris Commune of 1871, defensive barricaded positions inevitably vulnerable to disciplined regular troops. If you meant to win, you had to play the game by different rules – and maybe not always by polite rules.

The events of Easter Week are so well known and so well elaborated in a number of excellent narrative histories that they require only the briefest rehearsal here, with the emphasis on Collins's involvement. By Tuesday evening, the British army had isolated the GPO garrison by throwing a cordon around the city centre and occupying Capel Street. On Wednesday, the gunship *Helga II* moored in the Liffey at Butt Bridge and began an artillery assault on the Sackville Street area.

The *Helga II* was bought from the British by the Irish Free State in 1923 and renamed *Muirchú* (*Hound of the Sea*). She was sold for scrap in 1947 and sank off the Wexford coast on her delivery voyage.

In the afternoon, a small outpost of Éamon de Valera's garrison at Boland's Mills occupied buildings at Mount Street Bridge, from which position they ambushed British army reinforcements marching in from the ferry landing at Kingstown/ Dún Laoghaire and inflicted the heaviest casualties of the week on the British. Twelve volunteers, four of whom survived the action, were responsible for 230 British dead or wounded.

Outer garrisons fought bravely, especially that stationed at the South Dublin Union under the command of Éamonn Ceannt on the Friday, but it was, of course, hopeless. On the other hand, the garrison at Jacob's Biscuit Factory – a huge, industrial building invulnerable to everything except artillery, which the British had no intention of wasting on such a marginal position – saw hardly any action all week. As early as Thursday, it

Irish Volunteers inside the GPO.

was clear that the rising was coming to an end. Sackville Street was an inferno, with Clery's department store and the Imperial Hotel in flames. Even more alarmingly, Hoyle's oil refinery near North Earl Street was ablaze, which prompted Captain Brennan-Whitmore, on his own initiative, to abandon his barricaded position at the top of the street.

By Friday evening, it was clear that the GPO would have to be evacuated. They made for Moore Street. The British held the position at the far end of the street – at Great Britain (now Parnell) Street. One desperate frontal assault on that position, led by The O'Rahilly, was cut to pieces. One of those who died along with The O'Rahilly was Sean Hurley, Collins's cousin and oldest friend from West Cork and the man who had inducted him into the Irish Volunteers.

The O'Rahilly.

Captain Percival Lea-Wilson.

Collins, along with others from the GPO garrison, made it as far as 16 Moore Street. They could go no further. The final surrender came on the Saturday afternoon. When the formalities had been concluded, the Volunteers – now prisoners of the British – were marched up Sackville Street between troops with fixed bayonets and deposited in the gardens of the Rotunda maternity hospital in the centre of Rutland (now Parnell) Square. There was an irony in all this, for this was part of the campus in which the Irish Volunteers had been inaugurated in November 1913.

At first the prisoners were treated well by the British officers in charge, but that changed rather sharply when an Irish-born officer, Captain Percival Lea-Wilson, took charge. He appeared to have been drinking. At any rate, he immediately began to insult and harass the prisoners. One of them, Desmond Ryan, recalled that 'he strides around … threatening to have us all shot and telling us not to smoke, not to stand up and not to lie down and, if we want lavatories, use the beds provided and lie down in both.' He referred to the prisoners as animals. He snatched a document from the mortally ill Plunkett – it was his will – and brandished it in triumph.

Worst of all was his treatment of Tom Clarke. 'That old bastard is the commander-in-chief. He keeps a tobacco shop across the street. Nice general for your damned army.' Along with a number of others, Clarke was brought forward to the steps of the hospital and stripped naked. But Clarke was incapacitated by an old wound acquired in his long years in prison and he could not bend his arm fully. Lea-Wilson ripped off Clarke's jacket so abruptly that he caused the wound to re-open. Collins was appalled, and he was not alone.

However, the whirligig of time brings most things round. A few years later, in June 1920, Lea-Wilson was acting as a district inspector of the Royal Irish Constabulary (RIC) in Gorey, County Wexford. It was at the height of the War of Independence and by then Michael Collins was the man very much running the show, and coordinating a formidable intelligence and spying regime. He discovered Lea-Wilson's whereabouts and had him shot dead after buying himself a newspaper at Gorey railway station. It was sweet revenge for the brutal mistreatment of Clarke. There was an even more improbable twist to the tale: a few years later, Lea-Wilson's widow, a doctor, bought an old painting at auction; she gifted it to the Jesuits; years later, it was authenticated as a Caravaggio masterpiece, *The Taking of Christ*. It now hangs in the National Gallery of Ireland, one of the prized treasures of the collection.

Collins was among the large number of prisoners marched on the Sunday from the Rotunda Gardens to Richmond Barracks at Inchicore, in the south-western suburbs near Kilmainham Gaol, where the leaders of the rising were soon to face the firing squad in the Stonebreakers' Yard. En route, they had to endure the insults and hatred of the 'separation women', wives and widows of Irishmen serving on the Western Front: they were the second-largest cohort identified in a Dublin Corporation survey of inner-city tenement dwellers – after labourers – and they were not held in high esteem. In part, this was due to jealousy: the separation allowances they received from the War Office compared very well in comparative terms with labourers' wages, and partly because they had a deserved reputation for excessive drinking. For example, where there were 169 incidents of drunk and disorderly conduct

Caravaggio (Michelangelo Merisi), *The Taking of Christ,* 1602. This powerful work was painted at the height of Caravaggio's fame. Judas kisses and identifies Christ, who does not resist his arrest by the soldiers. The fleeing disciple on the left is St John the Evangelist.

involving men in the calendar year 1916, the equivalent number for women was 392. The suspicion was that the separation women were drinking their largesse.

These women provided the gauntlet that the Volunteers had to run as they were being escorted to Richmond Barracks. Pádraig Yeates, the best historian of this period in Dublin life, summed it up: 'What many prisoners probably did not know, and popular Dublin opinion quickly forgot, was that the rising coincided with the anniversary of the attack on Saint-Julien [in the 2nd Battle of Ypres], where the "Old Contemptibles" element of the Royal Dublin Fusiliers, including many working-class reservists, suffered such heavy losses. At least some of the women who abused the rebels would have been mothers, widows, wives, daughters or sisters of the dead and wounded.'

Once in Richmond Barracks, Collins had a lucky escape. The Volunteers were gathered in the gymnasium, with detectives from the G Division of the DMP – the section concerned with internal security – looking for known Fenians. It was they who made the first determination as to who was to go before a court martial, either to face a death sentence or a long stretch in penal servitude, and who might be treated less harshly. At first, Collins was identified

British soldiers loading prisoners into a truck in a Dublin street.

as one to face a more severe punishment. But when his name was called, he boldly walked across the room to join the group marked only for deportation – and got away with it. He had the devil's own good luck until the very end.

So he faced no court martial. The person who, more than anyone else, would break the back of British rule in Ireland, had got away with what was, in the circumstances, little more than a slap on the wrist.

Collins was later critical of the tactics of the rising and was the key figure in developing new guerrilla strategies to challenge British rule, but he never doubted the validity or necessity for the rising, setting out his views as follows:

'We [had become] the degraded and feeble imitators of our tyrants. English fashions, English material tastes and customs were introduced by the landlord class or adopted by them, and by a natural process they came to be associated in the minds of

British soldiers force entry to a rebel building during the Easter Rising. Early on Monday morning, 24 April 1916, roughly 1,200 Volunteers and Citizen Army members took over strongholds in Dublin city centre.

75

A military checkpoint in Dublin, with soldiers checking cars for arms and republican fugitives after the Easter Rising.

our people with gentility. The outward sign of a rise in the social scale became the extent to which we cast off everything which distinguished us as Irish and the success with which we imitated the enemy who despised us.'

He then contemplates the rising: 'Armed resistance was the indispensable factor in our struggle for freedom. It was never possible to us to be militarily strong, but we could be strong enough to make England uncomfortable … . While she explains the futility of force (by others) it is the only argument she listens to. For ourselves, it had that practical advantage, but it was above all other things the expression of our separate nationhood.

'It appeared at the time of the surrender to have failed, but that valiant effort and the martyrdoms which followed it finally awoke the sleeping spirit of Ireland.'

Sinn Féin prisoners at Richmond Barracks, 1916.

CHAPTER 4

Frongoch

'Let us be
judged for what
we attempted
rather than
for what we
achieved.'

Michael Collins

Collins was deported to England and deposited in Stafford jail on 1 May 1916. For most of that month, he and the other Irish detainees were held in solitary confinement, but as the regime was gradually relaxed they were permitted free association. The result was what one would expect from boisterous and frustrated young men: games of physical endurance, wrestling and a kind of leapfrog. All this suited Collins's vigorous nature. It was not just the hot-blooded, short-tempered side of his personality that the others noticed, but also the reflective side. He had books sent in from Ireland and he continued his lifelong habit of voracious reading.

Something else was evident at Stafford, which would dominate the rest of his life and how it was remembered. He possessed innate leadership skills; others looked to him as a source of decision and authority. In the confinement of prison, that need to be at the head of things, to make the running in things, which he had demonstrated even as a small boy playing games, now began to assert itself even more.

A few people in any group have this capacity naturally. Collins had it abundantly and he now had a context in which it could flourish. Following the executions of the 1916 leaders – news of

Michael Collins after release from Frongoch internment camp, Christmas 1916.

The execution of James Connolly.

which gradually reached Stafford and other jails around England where Irish prisoners were being detained – the leadership of advanced nationalism was open to a new generation. Mainstream nationalism in the form of the IPP under John Redmond had been weakened by the rising, but it was by no means dead, at least not yet.

None the less, the momentum was now, more than ever before, with the advanced element. The executions disgusted and outraged nationalist public opinion, not least the shooting of James Connolly, strapped into a chair because of an ankle wound acquired during the fighting, since turned gangrenous. Thus circumstanced, he faced the firing squad.

One of the most acute contemporary observers of 1916 was the novelist James Stephens, who lived through Easter Week in Dublin and has left us an invaluable eyewitness account of what he saw. In summing up his conclusions, he wrote the following prophetic passage:

Novelist James Stephens.

'The truth is that Ireland is not cowed. She is excited a little. She was not with the revolution, but in a few months she will

81

be, and her heart which was withering will be warmed by the knowledge that men thought her worth dying for.'

He was right. It didn't even take months. The speed with which public opinion began to turn can be measured in days. Just a few days after the Volunteers had to run the gauntlet of the separation women and others, a group of lesser prisoners, many of them to become close associates of Collins, were being marched from Kilmainham en route to jail in England when they were met with cheers and salutes from people on trams and in the streets.

What all this meant was that there was bound to be a generational change at the head of advanced nationalism and, furthermore, that there would be pressure to steer that advanced element towards the centre. This is substantially what happened over the next year or 18 months. But first, some serious thought was required as to how the nationalist demand could be rearticulated and carried forward. By incarcerating a lot of bright young men and allowing them free association, the British provided ideal conditions for a grand nationalist seminar.

There were just over 2,500 Irish prisoners scattered all around England in jails like Stafford. It was decided to consolidate them in one place as far as possible. The site chosen was a disused distillery in North Wales at a place called Frongoch, a few miles north of Bala. It now found itself home to somewhere between 1,500 and 2,000 Irish. It had been used as a German prisoner-of-war camp, and was filthy and rat-infested.

Frongoch camp parade.

Collins certainly did not care for it, for it seemed to rain all the time and he complained of the cold, even though this was high summer, or as high as summer got that year. In one letter, he described conditions in the camp: 'We sleep thirty in an 'ut [sic], the dimensions being 60 long, 16 wide and 10 foot high in the middle. Not too much room to spare!' There were two parts to the camp, north and south, with the south worse than the north and used by the authorities as a punishment station. It did not want for custom: from the start, the prisoners were cheerfully recalcitrant and challenged the disciplinary regime of the camp at every opportunity – it maintained morale.

It also led to the suicide of the camp doctor, who drowned himself in the local river having endured accusations of refusing medical assistance to difficult prisoners. The camp governor, Colonel F. A. Heygate Lambert, accused the prisoners of having hounded an innocent and dedicated professional man to his death. This was answered and declared a 'monstrous' accusation by the honorary secretary of the Prisoners' Committee, one Michael Collins. Once again, he was displaying his organisational ability, his love of structure and his tempestuous energy. He also displayed his ruthlessness: under his influence, the officer corps among the prisoners was reconstituted and stuffed with IRB men.

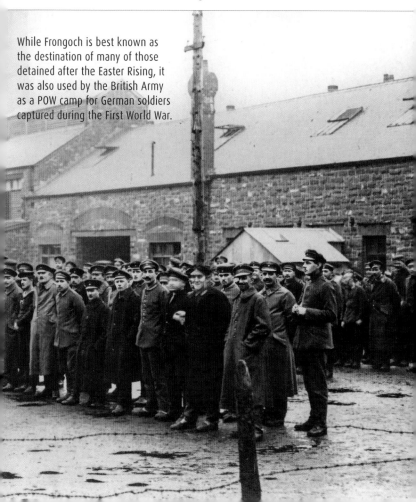

While Frongoch is best known as the destination of many of those detained after the Easter Rising, it was also used by the British Army as a POW camp for German soldiers captured during the First World War.

He also wrote up a piece of propaganda that was so overstated as to conditions in the camp that two diehard Fenians, Gerry Boland and Oscar Traynor, refused to sign it because of its untruths. True or not, Collins managed to get it out and it was published by a prisoners' dependants' fund in Cork, adding further to the charge of British ill-treatment of the Irish.

As it happened, a significant number of Munster men were assigned to Frongoch and they soon formed a clannish circle around Collins. They formed the nucleus of the famous 'revolutionary university' that Frongoch was fast becoming. In fact, conditions cannot have been anything as bad as Collins represented them in his propaganda piece. It was not an enclosed prison with walls and cells, like Stafford; it was an open campus and the men were able to organise athletic events to help run off the tedium of incarceration.

But it was for the mental rather than the physical endeavour that Frongoch was important. There were Irish language classes, cultural discussion groups, political seminars. Most of all, there was a rethink about the military strategy behind the Easter Rising. Gradually, there emerged a determination that a static defensive tactic such as that adopted during Easter Week was doomed to failure. Superior numbers, disciplined regular troops, and superior firepower would overwhelm it every time. Major John MacBride had said as much before his execution, drawing on his experience fighting for the Boers in the Second Boer War. The Boers had fought the British on the move, using their knowledge of the terrain and taking advantage of the huge distances in South Africa. It was a hit-and-run tactic.

It had worked well enough to give the British a very good run for their money. They were always going to win in the end, but it took them three years to do it against irregulars and then only by drawing on themselves the moral stain of inventing the modern concentration camp to incarcerate Boer women and children. These lessons were gradually absorbed in the discussions at Frongoch, and in all these reconsiderations Collins was central,

Major John MacBride, painted by Mick O'Dea.

87

so central, indeed, that he was elected head of the IRB in the camp. He was also instrumental in placing IRB men in positions of influence, so that when the prisoners were released, he had a fair claim to march out at the head of them.

It was in Frongoch that Collins finally impressed upon his contemporaries that mixture of cold-blooded mental calculation, boisterous physical presence and sheer charisma – force of personality – that brought him so many loyal followers and many (though fewer) resentful enemies in the coming years. What was clear beyond dispute was that this exceptional personality had a presence that attracted, cowed and repelled his contemporaries. These are qualities mysteriously distributed and given to few. O'Connell and Parnell had them; Bonaparte, pre-eminently, had them, and Collins – like Bonaparte – carried a field-marshal's baton, if only figuratively, before the age of 30. It is a struggle to recall that this man of cool mental

Drawing of the North Camp, Frongoch, 1917.

calculation and volcanic energy scaled the heights that he did without living to see his own 32nd birthday.

But so it was. And it was incubated and made manifest in Frongoch. It was there that Collins announced himself as the coming man.

He was also instrumental in ending the Frongoch regime. The damaging accounts of conditions in the camp – mendacious exaggerations and all – were picked up by sympathetic journalists on both sides of the Irish Sea as well as in the United States – to whose opinion Great Britain was especially sensitive, panting as it was to get the United States into the war and therefore conscious of the isolationist and deeply Anglophobic Irish-American lobby in the governing Democratic party, whom they did not wish to antagonise.

The upshot was that the British folded its hand. Just before Christmas 1916, the chief secretary for Ireland – a long-forgotten nonentity called Henry Duke – declared an amnesty. The gates of Frongoch were thrown open and the Irish prisoners walked out, free men, bound for Holyhead and the boat home to Ireland.

Frongoch was, in many ways, the making of Michael Collins. He had come back to Ireland from his nine years in London in January 1916. He had played a minor part in the drama of the Easter Rising and been extremely lucky to have got away with merely being deported to Wales rather than face a more severe punishment. But once there, his mixture of intellect and personality marked him as one of the key people – if not the key person – of the rising revolutionary generation. In Lewes jail in Sussex, the only surviving garrison commander from the rising, Éamon de Valera, was establishing a similar pre-eminence among the Irish prisoners there. These were the two names that would dominate the events of the coming years.

Their names – Collins and de Valera, the Big Fella and the Long Fella – are forever linked. In personality, they were utterly different. De Valera, ascetic and serpentine, was the more natural politician. Collins,

Éamon de Valera.

impatient with the theoretical hair-splitting to which De Valera was prone, was more the man of action. But, as was emerging in Frongoch, it was action with a thought-out strategy behind it. Whatever he was, Collins was not merely a swaggering gunman indifferent to ideas. His ideas about how the struggle for Irish freedom would best be carried forward were the product of a fertile, restless intellect.

Michael Collins in military uniform.

Up to this point, all Irish revolutionary nationalism had ever known was fiasco and heroic failure. Pearse had dressed it all up in an apostolic succession of mythical history that made a rosary of rebellions: 1641, 1798, 1848, 1867. The fact that the first one had nothing to do with political nationhood in the modern

91

'Of Pearse and Connolly I admire the latter the most. Connolly was a realist, Pearse the direct opposite. I would have followed Connolly to hell had such action been necessary. But I honestly doubt I would have followed Pearse … '

Michael Collins

sense – the idea had not been invented – and that the last two were little more than pathetic non-events was beside the point. Pearse had gifted the Irish revolutionary movement an enabling myth, and myths are important – often more potent than mere facts.

It was Collins who carried the movement beyond myth. The practical, finance Collins who could do trial balances and prepare balance sheets was impatient with heroic failure. Thus his coolness towards the memory of Pearse. Collins wanted to win, and so he had to figure out how a path to victory could be constructed. The Irish revolutionaries were up against the mightiest country in the world, possessed of an empire more far-flung than any in history. How were they to win?

They would have to fight differently, and they would have to fight dirty. Frongoch was the incubator in which these ideas took shape.

Colourised image of the surrender of Patrick Pearse to British forces, which ended the Easter Rising.

CHAPTER 5

The Prisoners Return

'He was an Irish patriot, true and fearless.'

Winston Churchill

Crowds waiting to meet prisoners released under the general amnesty.

The prisoners were free. They were escorted to Holyhead and put on the boat home. It landed at Kingstown/Dún Laoghaire, from where they entrained for the short rail journey into Dublin city. They detrained at Westland Row (now Pearse) station. When they had last marched through Dublin, they had been the victims of catcalls and insults. But now, in just seven months, all was transformed. Some of the men were shouldered aloft. They were carried through enthusiastic and approving crowds. What had caused this change? In part, it was a fulfilment of James Stephens's prescient prophecy. But the key vector had been the executions and the disgust that they engendered in the nationalist population. What of it if the leaders of the rising had been foolish dreamers and poets and literary men? They were Irish, and brave – and the English had put 15 of them up against a wall and shot them dead and hanged another one in London. Even if you had doubts about the wisdom of the rising, there was no denying the heroic courage of its leaders.

From the perspective of the British military commander in Ireland, Sir John Grenfell Maxwell, the rising had simply been an act of treachery and treason in time of war – and not any war, but the most existential struggle Britain had faced since Bonaparte a century earlier. It was a betrayal of country in a most critical moment and deserved only one punishment. Originally, 90 death sentences were decreed until Prime Minister Asquith belatedly took things in hand, came over from London and put a stop to the executions. From a military point of view, the executions were completely explicable – indeed, requiring no explanation at all, so obvious was the case. Politically, however, they were a disastrous misjudgement, as bad a misjudgement as Britain ever made in Ireland.

The point was that the rebels had not betrayed their country. They had fought to free it. Ireland, not Britain, was their country and they knew it and recognised no other. This understanding did not take long to seep into the wider nationalist consciousness. So, when the surviving prisoners – home from Britain – detrained at Westland Row, they were welcomed home to a country transformed.

Sir John Grenfell Maxwell.

Irish Republican Army
Adjutant General Gearóid
O'Sullivan.

Collins arrived on Christmas morning with his fellow Cork man Gearóid O'Sullivan, who had been the youngest officer serving in the GPO during the rising and had accordingly been honoured by being asked to raise the tricolour over the building on Easter Monday. He and Collins were to remain close to the very end, O'Sullivan becoming adjutant-general of the IRA under Collins's command. When he received the news of Collins's death, he simply broke down.

But that was almost six years away. Now, on Christmas Day 1916 in Dublin, Collins and O'Sullivan looked up some comrades in the city. But most of all, they drank. By the time they were done, Collins was in high spirits. He made his way to Kingsbridge (now Heuston) station, got on the train to Cork and fell into a deep sleep. He was free and happy and going home.

Collins's principal ambition on his return to Ireland was the rebuilding and strengthening of the IRB. On 19 February 1917, he took the first step in this direction when he was appointed Secretary of the Irish National Aid and Volunteers' Dependants' Fund. 'Anointed' might be the more appropriate verb, because he secured this position at the direct command of Mrs Kathleen Clarke. As the widow of Thomas Clarke, unrepentant Fenian and first signatory of the proclamation of the republic, as well as the sister of Ned Daly, another of the executed leaders of the rising, she commanded immense prestige and deference within the republican tradition.

Kathleen Clarke with sons (*left to right*) Tom, John and Emmet.

She clearly recognised in Collins some of the spirit of her husband and her brother. The fund that Collins was now to administer with his customary brisk efficiency was designed to offer material assistance to the families and relatives of

Kathleen Clarke, 1924.

those who died in the rising or were imprisoned in its aftermath. The source of the funds came from public subscriptions, but most of all from the United States, where a relief fund under the presidency of a descendant of Robert Emmet raised a substantial fund to be remitted to Dublin. This was done through Clan na Gael, the leading Irish-American support group for Irish revolutionary endeavour, in effect, the overseas branch of the IRB. In addition to the funds raised by the principal relief fund, the Clan added further monies raised through its own network.

Roger Casement (*left*) and John Devoy, in New York.

So now Michael Collins occupied a position in the Fenian firmament from which he could exercise influence. He established contacts with senior people on both sides of the Atlantic, few more important than John Devoy in New York, the key man in Clan na Gael. He set up an arms-smuggling network which would prove its worth in due time, sourcing materiel principally through Fenian contacts in Britain. His aim was to reconstitute the Irish Volunteers and the IRB following the losses in the rising.

But there was another aspect to all this. So far, Collins had shown himself to be an able administrator and a vigorous, yet cerebral, soldier. Just a few weeks before his appointment as administrator of the fund, he had dipped his toe in politics for the first time.

The British had dubbed the Easter rising the Sinn Féin rebellion, in the wholly mistaken belief that Arthur Griffith's noisy but marginal party had something to do with it. In fact, it was the work of a small, secret cabal within the IRB, which was itself operating within the Irish Volunteers. Not one of the leaders of the rising would have dreamed of taking Griffith into their confidence. He was hardly a republican at all, having been best known to the public for proposing a dual monarchy settlement for the Irish

problem along the lines of the Austro-Hungarian *Ausgleich* of 1867.
For republicans, any kind of monarchy was unacceptable.

None the less, the name Sinn Féin now stuck fast to all political
iterations of advanced nationalism in the aftermath of the rising.
Griffith, who had been rounded up and jailed by the British, was
released and resumed his position – for the moment – as party
leader. But it was a party quite unlike that which he had led before
the rising. The British misnomer was turning into a self-fulfilling
prophecy and Sinn Féin now became the big tent that held all
those radical nationalists who stood to the left of Redmond and
the IPP.

Their first opportunity arose as early as January 1917 when
there was a by-election in Roscommon North, necessitated by
the death of IPP veteran J. J. O'Kelly, a Parnellite who had held
the seat since 1880. He had had a colourful career, having fought
with the French Foreign Legion in Mexico, before deserting and
making his way to New York where he worked on James Gordon
Bennett's *New York Herald* and made friends in Fenian circles,
including John Devoy. He was on the military council of the IRB
for a while. On his return to Ireland, he worked as a journalist. In
his constituency, he was usually returned unopposed.

Now, in the first month of 1917, there would be no uncontested seat. Sinn Féin resolved to run a candidate. Their choice was none other than George Noble, Count Plunkett, father of the martyred Joseph. He had been cold-shouldered by some of his establishment associates because of his son's part in the rising and now he made his first, hesitant appearance on the public stage, under the Sinn Féin banner. Collins threw himself into the campaign

Lawrence Ginnell (wearing top hat) and Count and Countess Plunkett (back seat of car) at the Longford by-election, 9 May 1917.

with characteristic vigour and enthusiasm, approving completely of this political initiative. It was a chance to test the temperature of a deeply nationalist constituency, to amplify the message of advanced republican policy and to weaken the hold of the Irish Parliamentary Party. This latter was facilitated by a split in the non-Sinn Féin vote: the official party candidate, T. J. Devine, faced a challenge from an independent nationalist, Jasper Tully, a former MP and newspaper publisher who had been imprisoned along with Parnell in Kilmainham back in 1882.

The Count won handsomely, polling 3,022 to Devine's 1,708,

George Noble, Count Plunkett.

with poor Tully coming in last with 687. So Sinn Féin, on its first post-rising electoral outing, had secured an overall majority of votes cast (56 per cent). Prior to the election, Plunkett had not declared whether he would take his seat at Westminster if elected. One of the bedrock principles of Griffith's pre-rising Sinn Féin had been abstention from Westminster: Irish MPs should establish their own deliberative body in Dublin and refuse any legitimacy to a British parliament to legislate for Ireland. The post-rising republicans may not have had much time for Griffith's dual monarchy idea, but they thoroughly approved of abstentionism. They had stuck with Plunkett – perhaps *faute de mieux* – while he failed to declare himself on this cardinal issue. Now, in the wake of his victory, he did: he would not be going to Westminster to take his seat. That settled it. From now on, abstentionism from Westminster and the ambition to establish a separate parliament in Ireland became central to Sinn Féin's ambitions and dogma.

Collins's own summary of this by-election is interesting for a number of reasons, but in particular for his stated belief that the 1916 Rising was receding in the popular memory and the election rekindled support for its republican ideals, as well as his assertion that the main strategic goal was the displacement of the IPP by Sinn Féin. In short, this was a contest to help determine what the forward thrust of nationalism was to comprise.

'When the first by-election after the rising took place in North Roscommon in 1917, so much of the republic of Easter Week had been forgotten and so little had its teachings yet penetrated to the minds of the people, that, though the candidate was Count Plunkett, whose son had been martyred after the rising, he was returned only on the ground of his opposition to the Irish Party candidate.

'Abstention from attendance at the British parliament was the indispensable factor in the republican ideal – the repudiation of foreign government. But it was only after his election that the Count declared his intention not to go to Westminster, and the announcement was not received very enthusiastically by some of the more energetic of his supporters. They had returned a man, it was said, 'who did not intend to represent them anywhere'. Not only the people, but even some who had been engaged in the rising hardly grasped the new teaching.

'The election and others which followed were not won on the policy of upholding a republic, but on the challenge it made to the old Irish Party.'

This analysis is interesting, even allowing for an element of hindsight, in that Collins the republican acknowledged that the republic as an ideal was not the primary motivating factor that was driving this internal change – from the IPP to Sinn Féin – within the broader nationalist tent. When it came to the sticking place a few years later at the conclusion of the treaty, Collins took the most that was on offer, even though that was short of the full republican demand. Subsequent electoral tests were to justify that decision, and to endorse a view formed as early as the North Roscommon by-election.

Plunkett's victory in North Roscommon was quickly followed by another, even more consequential by-election, this time in the neighbouring constituency of Longford South. Once again, the IPP had held the seat, generally unopposed, since the 1880s. In 1917, the sitting member was one John

Count and Countess Plunkett.

'Hurrah for Plunkett,
Ring out the slogan call.
The Count's our man,
He leads the van for
Ireland over all.'

Canvassing slogan in North
Roscommon, February 1917.

107

Phillips, whose death occasioned the by-election. The party put up a good local candidate, Patrick McKenna, but Sinn Féin pulled what would later become known in Irish political parlance as a stroke – a bold-as-brass piece of cheek. They ran a prisoner in Lewes jail, Joe McGuinness – who was, incidentally, a very reluctant conscript to the cause, being encouraged in his reluctance by his Volunteer superior in the jail, Éamon de Valera. As the senior surviving garrison commander from 1916, de Valera already commanded an immense and growing prestige within the wider republican community. None the less, the men on the ground ran

McGuinness campaign car, South Longford by-election, 1917. McGuinness was in prison at this time in Lewes, England, for his part in the 1916 Rising.

McGUINNESS
IS WINNING

McGuinness under the Sinn Féin abstentionist banner but also under one of the greatest political slogans ever dreamt up: 'Put him in to get him out.'

They put him in. It was a close-run thing. McKenna was no pushover and McGuinness for obvious reasons could not canvass the constituency itself. None the less, when the poll was declared on 9 May he won, squeaking home by 1,493 votes to McKenna's 1,461, although there were suggestions of dirty work behind this short-head victory. In the physical absence of the Sinn Féin candidate, the party stalwarts had to muster for the campaign in Longford South. Collins was among them, ever more in the thick of things – his administration of the relief fund was already drawing glowing praise for its efficiency and emotional intelligence – and thus he found himself ensconced in the Greville Arms Hotel in Granard, County Longford.

The Greville Arms had been owned and run by Peter Kiernan and his wife Bridget, both of whom died within months of each other in 1908. They had had five surviving children, four of them daughters. The son, Laurence (Larry), was taken out of school early and established as head of the family business. He proved over time to be a successful provincial businessman and local

Harry Boland.

politician. One of the daughters, Helen, caught Collins's eye and it seems that he fell in love with her. It did not work out: she married a local solicitor. According to Frank O'Connor, Collins was distraught at this turn of events, but he soon set his cap at Helen's younger sister Catherine Brigid Kiernan, known ever after as Kitty. This time his affection was reciprocated, although there was a complicating factor, which would prove consequential in the coming years. Harry Boland, another IRB man and a 1916 veteran, was also in love with Kitty. Both of his brothers had been 'out' as well in 1916, with the result that the Bolands were fast becoming established as republican royalty, although they would hardly have phrased it thus. There were all the ingredients here for a tragic love triangle.

McGuinness's victory in Longford South was a blow to the British, who

could have excused Count Plunkett's win on the grounds that he was what we would now call a celebrity candidate, but no such mitigation could be advanced in the case of McGuinness. It was an even greater blow to the IPP, which had faced nationalist opposition for two elections in a row and lost them both (albeit the charge of intimidation of the returning officer in Longford was laid but never proved). One way or another, the party was never again going to have things its own way, as it had become accustomed to doing for so long. Even if McGuinness had lost – the first declaration suggested that he had, until the returning officer found, or contrived or was persuaded to find, some previously 'missing' ballots – it was clear that the tide was rising for Sinn Féin. Soon, de Valera would win in East Clare, W. T. Cosgrave in Kilkenny and Arthur Griffith in Cavan. The IPP won three by-elections as well but one was on a

Kitty Kiernan.

sympathy vote and two were in Ulster, where the Ancient Order of Hibernians was well organised and duly turned out the local vote in support of the old party.

Overall, however, the direction of electoral traffic was clear and it was running for Sinn Féin. By June 1917, all the remaining Irish prisoners had been released from British prisons. They included de Valera, who quickly established himself as the leader of the reconstituted Sinn Féin, Griffith selflessly standing aside to act as his deputy.

There followed a macabre tragedy that convulsed Ireland. Thomas Ashe was a teacher, originally from Tralee, County Kerry, formed in the classical mould of republican revolutionaries, with a background in the Gaelic League and the Volunteers. He commanded one of the very few Volunteer actions outside Dublin city during Easter Week 1916, successfully capturing four RIC barracks near Ashbourne in north County Dublin, for which he was court-martialled and sentenced to death, although the sentence was commuted to penal servitude for life. He was released in 1917 but was soon arrested again for making 'speeches calculated to cause disaffection'. For this offence, he was sentenced to one year with hard labour. He demanded political status and when this was denied, he and other republican prisoners in

Mountjoy jail in Dublin went on hunger strike. Ashe died on 25 September after forcible feeding.

His funeral five days later was an occasion for national mourning and emotion. It was in the grand tradition of nationalist funerals, except that this time the IRB were firmly in charge and Michael Collins was firmly in charge of the IRB. Collins was tasked with delivering the oration at the graveside. In its own way, it was as telling as Pearse's magnificent oratory at the grave of O'Donovan Rossa two years earlier. It was also as different from Pearse's oration as could be. Three volleys were fired over the coffin. Then Collins, in full Irish Volunteer uniform, stepped forward and declared: 'Nothing additional remains to be said. The volley which we have just heard is the only speech which it is proper to make above the grave of a dead Fenian.'

The funeral of Thomas Ashe, Dublin City Hall, 30 September 1917.

CHAPTER 6

Sinn
Féin
Redux

'I am a war man
in the day of
war, but I am
a peace man
in the day of
peace.'

Michael Collins

That brisk declaration over the coffin of Thomas Ashe was Michael Collins's arrival on the public stage. Hitherto, he had been well known in conspiratorial circles, admired by many if resented by a few. Now, for the first time, a wider public became aware of him. It would soon seem that his name was on every lip in Ireland – and not just in Ireland – but that had to start somewhere and it started at Thomas Ashe's funeral.

The following month, October 1917, there was a Sinn Féin árd-fheis (conference) at which the party was constituted anew. This was the moment when de Valera took over the presidency from Griffith, before being elected president of the Irish Volunteers the next day. For all practical purposes, this Sinn Féin was a new party. The fact that it retained the name of Griffith's pre-rising party was partly due to the mis-labelling by the British of all advanced nationalism under the Sinn Féin rubric. But this implied only partial continuity. Most obviously, this new Sinn Féin was avowedly republican and separatist, which Griffith's party had not been. However, there were aspects of Griffith's old programme that were carried through to the new party, abstentionism of course, but in particular his economic self-sufficiency, looking to build up Irish industries and manufactures behind tariff walls, as proposed by the German economist Friedrich List.

So, while the new party was republican in declaration, it was also a coalition between genuine republicans – Collins, de Valera and the Bolands – and those who remained closer to Griffith's original programme. De Valera managed to square this circle for the moment with a piece of intellectual conjuring – not the last time that remarkable mind would dance on the head of a pin – by proposing the formula that Sinn Féin aimed to secure a republic, following which the Irish people could choose by plebiscite the form of government they preferred. The party was abstentionist (from London) and utterly opposed to conscription. By December, just two months after this árd-fheis, Sinn Féin had attracted over 100,000 members. It was clearly the party of the future.

In a sad coda to all this, John Redmond died a few months later, worn out and bypassed by history, at the age of 62.

By now, Michael Collins had been elected to the executive of Sinn Féin and appointed adjutant-general of the Irish Volunteers. This was typical of how the advanced element, and especially the IRB, were consolidating their place at the heart of the new nationalist dispensation. It was by no means clear that they represented a majority of the new party; the old Griffith supporters were still numerous, and some of the more radical Home Rulers now inclined towards Sinn Féin, sensing the way the wind was blowing.

For instance, although Collins was elected to the executive of the party, he only won the last available place. The greatest number of votes went to Griffith's supporters, who dominated the top of the poll. But the muscle and the ambition lay with the advanced men. Collins's appointment as adjutant-general of the Volunteers took place in secret, at Jones Road in Drumcondra – at what is now Croke Park, the headquarters of the GAA – and was dominated by the IRB element. They not only secured Collins his new position but saw to the election of two other IRB men to key positions. Diarmuid Lynch became director of communications and Sean MacGarry was elected general secretary.

These internal tensions, most evident in Sinn Féin, between those who were full-blooded republicans and those who were not also concealed potential differences between those who were out-and-out physical force men and those who were open to political dialogue. For a long time, it was assumed that Collins was one of the former; it was certainly a strong element of his personality, but that old practical, organised, finance Collins was always there lurking somewhere. He would surprise many in due time.

These potential conflicts would, in time, produce splits and enmities that were tragic and destructive. But for now, as 1917 turned into 1918, it was a glad, confident morning for the newly constituted national movement. With his feet firmly established in the higher reaches of both the political and military sides of the movement, Michael Collins was a public figure of growing consequence. He had just turned 27 years of age.

Michael Collins, portrait by Irish artist Seamas Culligan.

Michael O'Hanrahan.

'We did not initiate the war; nor were we allowed to choose the battleground.'

Michael Collins

You just take to some people and Collins took to Ned Broy from the first. They met in March 1918. Broy was three years older than Collins and a member of the G Division of the Dublin Metropolitan Police (DMP), holding the rank of detective sergeant. He was a clerk in the intelligence division, with access to sensitive documents. He was also a nationalist, hailing originally from Rathangan, County Kildare, where old memories were kept warm. Atrocities committed by the yeomanry in 1798 had not been forgotten. This background in a community that had a historic resentment of British rule rubbed off on Broy, in particular in the months of heightened tension following the Easter Rising.

He began to develop modest contacts among republicans in the second half of 1916 and it was through these contacts that he and Collins eventually came to meet in March 1918. Broy was a keen athlete, something that he shared with Collins. One way or another, they seem to have trusted each other from the beginning. Broy explained to Collins how the DMP's intelligence system worked and how the capital's police force was structured.

Broy was running huge risks but he was canny. He generally operated at one or two removes, taking care not to be seen in obviously republican locales or addresses. He used intermediaries such as the family of Michael O'Hanrahan. Wexford-born O'Hanrahan had been part of the Jacob's Factory garrison during the 1916 Rising; despite being at best third-in-command, he was executed – a glaring demonstration of how capricious the British death sentences could be, considering the number of people obviously senior to O'Hanrahan whose lives had been spared. His family, who had a business in central Dublin, had every reason to feel bitter. They were one of the conduits for information that Broy developed.

Broy was sincere in his desire to help republicans, but republicans were understandably cautious about investing trust in a G-Man who was most likely an agent provocateur. In fact, he was no such thing, but it took a leap of faith to trust him, as Collins did. It soon materialised that Broy was not as much of a rarity as might be imagined. There were other policemen in the Castle regime who were sympathetic to the republican cause. Two of them, David Neligan and Joe Kavanagh, were soon in touch with Collins. Neligan, in particular, was probably second in importance to Broy in sustaining Collins's intelligence network over the next few years.

Broy was stationed at Great Brunswick (now Pearse) Street police station. One evening, in a spectacular piece of cheek, he got Collins and another Volunteer into the station and for a few hours the two republicans had the chance to examine some of the most sensitive political files in the city. A subsequent security leak almost had disastrous consequences, as it became clear that there was an informant somewhere in G Division, whose dispersed files were now centralised in Dublin Castle, where Broy had no access to them. None the less, he got away with it, as did the growing number of DMP men who were now part of Collins's network.

That network in time extended to sympathisers all over the city, including people in outwardly respectable and unimpeachable occupations, such as Thomas Gay, a librarian in the Capel Street branch of the city library system. Various businesses and commercial outlets were used as quick drop-off points. Harry

Boland was a tailor by trade and had a shop in Middle Abbey Street; that came in handy. Other businesses of the sort that would seldom arouse suspicion were also used.

It is worth recalling that, as all this was going on and Collins was building up his subversive network, the First World War was still raging. It was not going well for the Allies. True, they had at last got the Americans into the war on their side but it wasn't clear how soon they could be deployed, or how many of them there might be, or whether they would prove to be any good in the field. All these questions were answered in time, but in the early months of 1918 they were not yet a factor in the military equation. What was material was the mighty German spring offensive all along the Western Front that began on 21 March 1918. Ludendorff aimed to deliver one final knock-out blow to the Allies before the Americans could be deployed, something that he considered potentially fatal – as it was to prove in fact – to the German cause. The advance initially proved a spectacular success but then stalled, and by the time it had stalled in late June and early July, the Americans were deployed for the first time at battles such as Cantigny (28 May) and Chateau-Thierry (31 May).

The initial success of the German spring offensive in March and April threw the government of Lloyd George into a panic. On 9 April, it introduced a Military Service Bill to extend conscription to Ireland – to make good the losses caused not just by the spring offensive but also by the horrific carnage at Passchendaele the previous autumn. It passed the House of Commons in seven days. John Dillon, who had succeeded Redmond as leader of the IPP, withdrew his members from parliament in protest. He had little choice, given the strength of public feeling in Ireland in opposition to conscription. However, in doing so, he tacitly conceded Sinn Féin's abstentionist point.

As much as anything else, it was the threat of conscription – in the event, it was never carried out, as the war finally turned for the Allies, and decisively, in the summer – that finally broke the back of British rule in nationalist Ireland. Any residual legitimacy drained away. Suddenly, all shades of Irish

Anti-conscription poster.

nationalist opinion united in opposition to the proposal, including crucially the Catholic hierarchy. A pledge to oppose conscription was signed by nearly two million people across the country on 21 April: the wording had been settled by none other than Éamon de Valera, leader of Sinn Féin and president of the Irish Volunteers, now setting himself unambiguously at the head of his nation.

It quickly became clear to the British government that the plan was unenforceable. There was a general strike on 23 April. There

were demonstrations. It was evident that any attempt to stuff conscription down the throats of the Irish would result in massive civil disobedience and violence, probably necessitating martial law. It simply wasn't worth it. Besides, while Lloyd George and his cabinet were mulling over all this, the military situation began to ease as the Germans stalled and the US army began to fight.

Arthur Griffith and Éamon de Valera at the Anti-Conscription Conference, Dublin, 1918.

But, at the height of the British panic, in late April and early May, they made a colossal error. On 8 May, there appeared a story in *The Times*, always reliably malevolent and mendacious where Irish nationalism was concerned, to the effect that the British government had evidence of collusion between Sinn Féin and the Germans. This was the famous 'German Plot', a pure concoction. The source was attributed to Sir Edward Carson, the provenance of which should have made the journalists suspicious.

Three days later, a new lord lieutenant arrived in Ireland. This was John, Viscount French, born in England of an Anglo-Irish family and first commander-in-chief of the British Expeditionary Force at the start of the war. He was in no doubt at all about the validity of the German Plot, announcing shortly after his arrival in

Caricature of General John French from *Vanity Fair* in 1900.

Dublin that 'certain subjects … domiciled in Ireland, had entered into treasonable communication with the German enemy'. He furnished no evidence in support of this contention, for the excellent reason that there was none to be had. Later on, he imposed martial law on most of the south and west of the country.

The lack of evidence did not stop the authorities from embarking on a round-up of troublemakers. On 17–18 May, almost the entire leadership of Sinn Féin were detained. But not Michael Collins. On 15 May, two days before the round-up, Ned Broy had furnished Collins with a list of those targeted. At a meeting of the Volunteer executive, Collins shared this information with his colleagues, warning them not to go home that night. Most ignored this warning, went home and were duly picked up. Collins cycled out to the northern suburb of Clontarf to warn Seán McGarry, but arrived only to

Eamon 'Ned' Broy in Garda uniform.

Constance Markievicz in a studio pose.

find that he had been arrested already. Collins decided that the British would hardly raid the same house twice on the same night, so he decided to stay in McGarry's place.

As had happened after the 1916 Rising, the removal of major figures from the scene opened the door for those still active. This brought Collins, still out and about, even more to the fore. The Great War ended in November and a UK general election was called for the following month. Collins, along with Harry Boland, made sure that the Sinn Féin candidate list was dominated by advanced IRB men, and the occasional woman like Constance Markievicz (this was still an overwhelmingly masculine world). The result was revolutionary. Sinn Féin triumphed over the IPP, which was reduced to a remnant. There was talk of intimidation in some places, and no doubt there was some. But the overall result was beyond dispute or the reach of even the most intimidatory tactics.

Sinn Féin won 73 of Ireland's 105 seats; the IPP won 6, 5 of them in Ulster. Sinn Féin won 27 uncontested seats, including Collins's own in Cork South. It was, as much as anything, a generational and a class revolution. The recently enacted Representation of the People Act 1918 had hugely extended the electoral franchise in the United Kingdom, more than doubling the electorate overall and enfranchising all males over 21 without any requirement to own property; it also enfranchised all women over 30, but with minor property requirements attached. The net effect was to give a new generation the vote. In Ireland, they voted for Sinn Féin.

It was now the unequivocal voice of Irish nationalist ambition, articulated in republican, separatist terms. The nationalist demand had been hugely raised. Home Rule was no longer enough. The demand was for separation from Britain and the establishment of a sovereign, independent Irish state. There was, of course, no question of the 73 successful Sinn Féin MPs taking their seats at Westminster (nor did the 6 IPP MPs bother either, seeing that their jig was up). Instead, they resolved to form their own assembly in Dublin.

They did this on 21 January 1919, constituting themselves (or as many of them as were not in English jails) as Dáil Éireann or the Irish Assembly, a lower house similar to the House of Commons or the US House of Representatives or the Assemblée Nationale. On the same day, however, the first shots were fired in what, ever after, was known as the War of Independence. At a quarry at Soloheadbeg in County Tipperary, a lonely place a little north of Tipperary town, the South Tipperary Brigade of the Irish Republican Army – as the Irish Volunteers were coming to style themselves – held up two RIC policemen accompanying a cargo of gelignite from Tipperary town to the quarry. The intention was to capture the explosive without violence.

That is not what happened. The two policemen refused to release the gelignite and were shot dead for their pains. They were the first police casualties since 1916. Their names were James McDonnell and Patrick O'Connell, both Catholics; McDonnell was 50 years of age and the father of five children; O'Connell was unmarried. Both were popular in the neighbourhood. The IRA brigade was led by Seamus Robinson, Dan Breen, Sean Hogan and Sean Treacy. The attack was not sanctioned by headquarters in Dublin, from which the South Tipperary unit was largely estranged. Richard Mulcahy, the chief of staff, was outraged. Collins, too, was unimpressed,

POLICE NOTICE.
£1000 REWARD
WANTED FOR MURDER IN IRELAND.

DANIEL BREEN
(calls himself Commandant of the Third Tipperary Brigade)

Age 27, 5 feet 7 inches in height, bronzed complexion, dark hair (long in front), grey eyes, short cocked nose, stout build, weight about 12 stone, clean shaven; sulky bulldog appearance; looks rather like a blacksmith coming from work; wears cap pulled well down over face.

Reward poster for Daniel Breen.

Opposite: The first Dáil Éireann.

Richard Mulcahy.

seeing quite correctly that the South Tipperary brigade was really a freelance operation; moreover, there was no IRB presence there.

So none of the structural restraints so dear to Collins's organisational mind had any presence at Soloheadbeg. None the less, it has entered the Irish historical consciousness as a kind of foundation moment. The War of Independence is, rightly or wrongly, dated from this event. It was, in some ways, all too typical of what followed. The war was disproportionately reliant on local commanders of energy rather than on central direction and command from the likes of Mulcahy and Collins in Dublin. This accounts for the episodic nature of the war and the fact that some counties and districts made very little contribution to the overall effort, for want of good, enterprising local commanders.

One of Sinn Féin's declared ambitions in the general election had been that Dáil Éireann should appeal to the international conference in Paris that gathered to settle the world order in the wake of the First World War. It resolved to send delegates there in the hope of getting a hearing for Irish independence in conformity with Woodrow Wilson's famous Fourteen Points, which included the declared right of the freedom of small nations. The delegates were duly dispatched but did not get a hearing. The United Kingdom had been victorious in the war and had little time for Wilsonian guff; the small nations stuff might be fine for countries emerging from the wreckage of the Central Powers, but not for a constituent part of an Allied victor. Besides, Wilson was an Anglophile. But the Paris conference also engaged the attention and energy of David Lloyd George for most of 1919 and he had insufficient time to give to his back door, Ireland. But Ireland was about to run out of his control.

Collins's summary of the revolutionary years now beginning is worth recording. Note the legalism and the focus on England – the cultural other – rather than on Britain, and the emphasis placed once more on the consent of the governed. The word 'republic' is absent, hardly an oversight.

'Ireland's story from 1918 to 1921 may be summed up as the story of a struggle between our determination to govern ourselves and to get rid of the British government and the British determination to prevent us from doing either. It was a struggle between two rival governments, the one an Irish government resting on the will of the people and the other an alien government depending for its existence upon military force – the one gathering more and more authority, the other steadily losing ground and growing ever more desperate and unscrupulous. All the history of the three years must be read in the light of that fact.

'Ireland had never acquiesced in government by England. Gone for ever were policies which were a tacit admission that a foreign government could bestow freedom, or a measure of freedom, upon a nation that had never surrendered its national claim.

'We could take our freedom. We would set up a government of our own and defend it. We would take the government out of the hands of the foreigner who had no right to it, and who could exercise it only by force.

'A war was being waged by England and her allies in defence, it was said, of the freedom of small nationalities, to establish in such nations "the reign of law based upon the consent of the governed".

We, too, proposed to establish in Ireland "the reign of law based upon the consent of the governed".'

British soldiers seal off parts of Dublin as they search for hidden armaments on 21 January 1921.

CHAPTER 7

Politics & Guns

'The real riches of the Irish nation will be the men and women of the Irish nation.'

Michael Collins

The war quickly acquired a stuttering momentum of its own. In the early months of 1919, it was principally concentrated in Tipperary and neighbouring counties, although in late March there was a shooting in Westport, County Mayo, a county that otherwise saw relatively little action during the war. A resident magistrate, J. C. Milling, was shot and died shortly afterwards. It is unclear whether this action was on directions from Dublin HQ – it seems unlikely on balance – but it marked the first lethal attack on the civil arm of British legal administration.

In May, the South Tipperary brigade were back in action. At a railway station at Knocklong, County Limerick – just across the county boundary – Dan Breen and Sean Treacy held up a train that was carrying their colleague Sean Hogan under capture from Thurles to Cork. The train was headed for Limerick Junction, down the line, where the transfer to the Cork line could be effected. But Limerick Junction was too big and too exposed for a job such as this, so they decided to make their attempt at Knocklong. Hogan had carelessly returned home after Soloheadbeg – the rest of them had gone on the run, staying in safe houses – and was captured. The rescue worked; Hogan was freed, but Treacy and Breen were both wounded. More seriously, two more RIC men died.

These brave, if reckless, actions had the effect of increasing the British military presence in County Tipperary. It was declared a military area, and while this certainly retarded the further development of a disciplined republican military structure in the county, and one hopefully amenable to central direction from Dublin HQ, it did not bring it to a complete halt. Other policemen were shot, most notably District Inspector Hunt of the RIC.

Dan Breen's APPEAL

Dan Breen's appeal to His Old Comrades now in the Free State Army.

COMRADES!

Dan Breen's appeal to Free State troops.

At local level, and especially in County Tipperary, IRA commanders had been harassing the RIC for some time before the Dáil formally passed a motion authorising a boycott of the force in April 1919, in effect a retroactive legalisation of Soloheadbeg and an attempt to suggest some civilian control over the local military. Then, on 23 June, Hunt was shot dead in cold blood and in broad daylight in the Market Square, Thurles, the most senior police officer to die in the early months of the war. The IRA man who killed him was called Jim Stapleton. Neither he nor any of his accomplices wore any disguise.

No one testified against Stapleton, and it is too easy to put this down simply to intimidation, although it was a factor. But as one witness recalled: 'The crowd jeered and there were cries of "Up the Republic".' There was not the least sympathy for the dead man; he had been unpopular locally and was believed to have damaging information on the Knocklong affair. Public bodies passed no resolutions. As the same witness recalled: 'Scarcely a blind was drawn on the day of the funeral.'

All these incidents took place in the first few months of the war before the really rough stuff had started. But they were indicative of a palpable shift in public mood. The actions of the IRA were invested with legitimacy, which was progressively withdrawn – along with human sympathy – from the representatives of the crown. After Knocklong, both Treacy and Breen made their way to Dublin while nursing their wounds. There, they finally met up with Collins, who put them to work as part of his emerging squad. They were the kind of desperados he could find a use for, even if he could not always trust them to maintain discipline.

By now, Collins had masterminded a coup that burnished his growing legend. He had 'sprung' Éamon de Valera from Lincoln jail in England, where he had been held since his capture in connection with the German Plot. Also in Lincoln were Sean Mulroy and Seán McGarry – the same McGarry in whose house in Clontarf Collins had spent the night of the German Plot raids. De Valera had managed to make a wax impression of the jail's master key while doing duty as an altar server at Mass. He had borrowed the prison chaplain's master key and used melted candle wax from the altar to make the impression. The wax impression was smuggled out and eventually reached Collins. A key was made from it and returned to Lincoln concealed in a cake. It didn't work. They tried again, this time successfully.

Éamon de Valera returning from Lincoln jail.

On 3 February 1919, Collins and Gerry Boland were waiting outside the gates of Lincoln Jail when de Valera, Mulroy and McGarry opened every door and gate in the place, walked out, and were spirited away into the night. It was an extraordinary propaganda success for the republican movement. De Valera was lodged in Manchester with some of Collins's IRB associates – people for whom de Valera would, in the ordinary way of things, have little time, being averse to secret societies in general because of religious scruple. He was glad of them now. He was smuggled back to Dublin and immediately began to make plans to carry the republican cause to the United States.

The great pandemic of the Spanish Flu brought the release of the remaining German Plot prisoners a few weeks later, following the death of one of their number from the disease.

In April, the emphasis moved to politics. At the start of the month, the Dáil convened for the second time. De Valera, predictably, was elected President. Michael Collins was appointed Minister for Finance by de Valera. By this time, he was on the run, having reneged on a bail bond. Besides, the British authorities were now well aware of him and regarded him, quite correctly, as a prize catch. It made all that followed even more remarkable.

Collins now found himself simultaneously director of operations and adjutant-general of the IRA, the effective cortex of a sporadic guerrilla war, and Minister for Finance in a shadow administration tasked with raising a national loan in support of a state that had, as yet, no existence in international law and that was regarded as illegal by the nominal sovereign power. The entire story of the shadow or parallel government run by Sinn Féin is a tale of the improbable, but it had a genuine social presence, most visibly in the case of the Dáil courts system which replaced the crown courts in many parts of the country and whose judgments and determinations were accepted by the people. A more telling indication of the moral legitimacy of the republican project it would be hard to find.

This parallel government system – run by men themselves on the run – achieved wonders. Its moral force was at least as persuasive as anything the IRA did. But there's a glamour to guns that civilians can't match. Inevitably these revolutionary years are remembered in the nationalist consciousness not in terms of the shadow administration or the shadow legal system or the various non-violent prison protests – of which Terence MacSwiney's hunger strike to death was the most dramatic example – but as the War of Independence. That was, at best, half the story. The non-violent side of the struggle caught liberal British and international public opinion just as much as did the doings of the IRA.

But all this required money, and finding the money was now Collins's job. In September 1919, he launched the national loan drive. He administered the whole thing himself, even down to the clerkly details of personally issuing receipts for monies pledged. Once again, his administrative genius displayed itself. The loan drive needed publicity and Collins and Sinn Féin did not have the mainstream press on their side; nor did they have the moral influence of the Catholic hierarchy in support – the Church, as ever, treading very cautiously where anything deemed illegal was concerned. None the less, the loan drive raised almost £400,000 in short order, a sum all the more impressive when one recalls that republicans drew relatively little support from wealthy sections of the community.

A drive in the United States raised millions of dollars, enough of which found its way back to Ireland to augment Collins's remarkable effort. It was, of course, never enough to finance a complete parallel administration, which wouldn't have been possible once the war hotted up in earnest and the British began to fight dirty. It was enough to keep the rickety show on the road.

The funeral procession of Terence MacSwiney outside St George's Cathedral, Southwark, London, 28 October 1920.

Michael Collins is rightly remembered as the man who, more than anyone else, broke the back of the British police and security apparatus in Ireland. He should also be remembered for this astonishing administrative achievement, which anchored a political project that gave the Irish state *in utero* a moral legitimacy that no amount of gunplay could have achieved.

In June 1919, just a few months out of Lincoln Jail, de Valera went to the United States. He wanted to mobilise Irish-American

John W. Goff, Daniel Florence Cohalan, Éamon de Valera and John Devoy at the Waldorf Astoria, New York City, in March 1919, to commemorate de Valera's campaign for Irish independence in the United States.

opinion behind the Irish republican cause, raise funds and try to influence, as much as possible, the policies of the American government towards Ireland. He was to spend 18 months there. The visit was a propaganda success but it also got de Valera entangled in the endless and incomprehensible internecine quarrels of the Irish-Americans.

In the course of that summer, with de Valera in America, Collins was elected President of the Supreme Council of the IRB. In addition to the various formal and public offices he held, he was at the apex of a secret society without which the history of Irish republicanism over the preceding 60 years would have been vastly different. The IRB was the hard centre of the separatist movement, but it was also, of its nature, a potential source of division within that movement. IRB men, not least Collins himself, felt that they represented a militant, active, fighting elite and were inclined to have little patience with more temporising, purely political figures in Sinn Féin. These opposites were not obvious in the summer of 1919, but they would become material later.

Its ruthlessness, and Collins's, soon showed. Collins's evening in Great Brunswick Street DMP station in April 1919 had revealed to him the workings of the entire police and security apparatus.

It also gave him names, in particular the names of G-men in the DMP who represented, in his eyes, the front line of the enemy. He arranged for some of these men to be challenged and warned off an over-zealous performance of their duties. Most did not listen, thinking this little more than bluff and bluster.

How mistaken those judgements were was made clear on 31 July. Detective Patrick Smyth of G Division was killed by Collins's men in the north Dublin suburb of Drumcondra. Smyth was a stubborn man, determined to do his duty according to his own lights, which included disclosing to his superiors the contents of incriminating papers found on the person of Piaras Béaslaí TD, who had been arrested for making a seditious speech. He had been specifically warned against doing this by Collins's men, whom he regarded as 'young scuts'. A group of republican assassins under the direction of Collins waylaid 'The Dog' Smyth, as he was unhappily known, near his home in Millmount Avenue. There was an exchange of gunfire – Smyth went down fighting, but he went down all the same.

Then, on 12 September, Detective Inspector John Hoey, another G-man, was shot dead near that same Great Brunswick Street police station in which Collins had spent so many fruitful hours on that evening in the previous April. In many respects, Hoey was a marked man, for it was known that he was the one who had identified Seán MacDermott in the wake of the Easter Rising, which had been as good as a death sentence.

In effect, these were the first outings for what became known as the Squad. Although it was not yet formally established – that did not happen until 19 September – the killing of Smyth and Hoey

Paddy Daly.

meant that it already existed in reality. Now it was formalised at a meeting in Parnell Square; it was hardly a coincidence that it was the same address at which meetings of the Keating Branch of the Gaelic League took place. At first, they numbered nine, to which three more were added a few months later, giving them the sobriquet of the Twelve Apostles.

They were assassins, a hit squad, pure and simple. It was made plain to them from the outset that this was their business and that anyone who had moral qualms about taking human life had better withdraw now. None of them was under any illusion as to their purpose. Their immediate targets were the G-men. Some had been neutralised and intimidated into passivity by warnings, but the more determined and recalcitrant, like Patrick Smyth, were killed.

The G Division of the Dublin Metropolitan Police was the central nervous system of the entire British security apparatus in Ireland. By the end of 1919 and early 1920, the G Division was effectively emasculated. Men could be replaced but their priceless and sensitive knowledge could not. Every previous Irish separatist conspiracy had been riddled with informers and often compromised by alcohol. Collins was determined that the conduit for information would be eliminated – thus the destruction of the G-men – and also ensured that the Squad were temperate. There would be no *ex post facto* bragging in bars with tongues loosened by drink. These were proper, deadly, puritan revolutionaries.

District Officer Johnny Barton was killed in late November. A double agent named Molloy went the same way. In a few months, Collins's men had terrorised the DMP. A Detective Redmond was summoned from Belfast to stiffen the force's backbone and specifically to capture Collins, by now easily the most wanted man in Ireland. He too was shot. In 1920, a parallel campaign against RIC barracks in the countryside, which resulted in the abandonment of many of them, robbed the British of their eyes and ears outside the capital.

By now Sinn Féin had been declared an illegal organisation and the Dáil

'We must be true to our ideal if we are to achieve anything worthy.'

Michael Collins

proscribed, taking the political side of the movement largely out of the equation. This, combined with de Valera's absence in America, meant that Collins was now the central figure in the republican struggle. He had already broken the back of the British security state in a very short time. In December, members of the Squad, augmented by Breen and Treacy from Tipperary who had occasional walk-on parts in these transactions, almost pulled off a major sensation. They attempted to assassinate the Lord Lieutenant, French, in an ambush at the Ashtown gate entrance to the Phoenix Park in Dublin. The effort was botched; French survived, although Lieutenant Martin Savage of the IRA died in the gunfight that ensued.

And so 1919 yielded to 1920. By now, Lloyd George was back from the peace conference in Paris and able to devote his energy once again to domestic matters. None were more urgent than Ireland, where the very sinews of British rule were being weakened by Collins's ruthless, murderous campaign. While the Squad did not operate outside Dublin, their methods were echoed by local units of the IRA and had a devastating effect on RIC membership, and even more on recruitment. The police were quietly and fearfully disappearing from the Irish countryside.

It was a testimony to the galvanising energy and genius of Lloyd George that so much of this drift from British authority had occurred while he was otherwise engaged. Now he was back and he resolved to take the matter in hand. He had a choice: send in the army or augment the police. He chose the latter. On 25 March 1920, there arrived in Ireland the first contingent of the police auxiliary body known ever after as the Black and Tans. Because of a shortage of police uniform material, they wore the bottle-green jackets of the RIC and the khaki trousers of the British army. To many Irish eyes, they looked uncannily like the hunting pinks of the famous County Limerick hunt, the Scarteen Black and Tans: thus the name stuck. Although they contained some decent men – even some IRA leaders were prepared to allow as much – they were for the greater part undisciplined and extremely violent, many of them drunk; they quickly acquired a well-deserved reputation for vicious brutality against civilians and induced despair among the officers to whom they nominally answered.

They were for the most part a reactive outfit. If the IRA sustained an action, the Tans would react as often as not by shooting up the entire district, to intimidate such civilian support as there was for the republicans – which was usually plenty. They were further reinforced in July by the arrival of the Auxiliary

Police Forces, generally known simply as the Auxiliaries or the Auxies. They were given a free hand under repressive emergency legislation and were regarded in the eyes of the Irish populace as indistinguishable from the Black and Tans. Between them, they were a stain on the name of Britain, causing Lloyd George to boast that 'we have murder by the throat', a boast that was soon rendered very hollow indeed.

If Lloyd George was deluding himself, Collins was not much better. Perhaps in an attempt to assuage a guilty conscience, he declared that:

'In the first two years [1919 and 1920] all violence was the work of the British armed forces who in their efforts at suppression murdered fifteen Irishmen and wounded nearly 400 men, women and children. Meetings were broken up everywhere. National newspapers were suppressed. Over 1,000 men and women were arrested for political offences, usually of the most trivial nature. Seventy-seven of the national leaders were deported. *No police were killed during those two years* [author's italics]. The only disorder and bloodshed were the work of the British forces.'

This ignored the fact
that the first two to die in
the War of Independence
were policemen and that the
systematic elimination of many
others over that period of time
was expressly on the orders of
Collins himself. He could have
pleaded terrible necessity, this
being the only means to bring
British rule in Ireland to its
knees, but to deny it outright
was extraordinary. No person
in Ireland was in a better
position to know the truth of
the violence. No one was in a
weaker position to deny it.

A Black and Tan
auxiliary stands guard.

CHAPTER 8

The War Intensifies

'We fought in
a way we had
never fought
before, and
Ireland won
a victory she
had never won
before.'

Michael Collins

The period from the beginning of 1920 until the Anglo-Irish Truce of July 1921 was dominated by military affairs. On the republican side, that meant that Collins was in charge. He was the military strategist and had the necessary ruthlessness to follow through on the logic of the situation. Ned Broy had opened his eyes to the means by which British power was sustained in Ireland. Collins drew a grim but logical conclusion from this knowledge. In some ways, it could be represented as a classic Fenian analysis, which it was, but never before had one leading Fenian demonstrated his unique mixture of fierce intelligence, pitiless logic and the sheer force of personality required to get the job done. No one close to him – including those bruised by his bullying and hectoring – denied that, at this moment, he was a commanding figure.

Collins's ability to cycle around Dublin undetected, despite frequently being stopped at checkpoints, became the stuff of legend and burnished his reputation as a sort of Hibernian scarlet pimpernel. It seemed to help that he was always well dressed – again, it had been Broy who had tipped him off in this regard – because a well-groomed, neat, professional-looking man would make an unlikely revolutionary in the eyes of the authorities.

It was in these 18 months from early 1920 on that the military struggle was most concentrated. Lloyd George, home from Paris and spooked by the near assassination of the viceroy, upped the British response to the IRA campaign. This saw the arrival of the Black and Tans and, a little later, of the Auxiliaries. Meanwhile, the Irish side increased its effort.

There was a quite conscious assault on the RIC presence in the countryside. It worked as well as it did because the force, like all institutions of the crown in nationalist Ireland, lacked legitimacy. As often as not, individual policemen were well regarded by their local community. But it was

David Lloyd George.

Ernie O'Malley.

increasingly the uniform that failed them. This campaign had Collins's full support. Just how much direction he was able to give it will always be an open question. He was beyond any doubt the principal strategist behind the IRA campaign, but the sporadic nature of the war was the consequence of relying on vigorous local commanders, who were capable of acting on their own initiative.

So Michael Collins was crucial to the execution of the whole campaign, but exactly how crucial is impossible to measure with complete accuracy. Take the case of one outstanding IRA commander, Ernie O'Malley. He worked closely with Collins, helping to organise IRA units in various counties. Collins trusted him sufficiently to send him to London on an arms-buying mission. In February 1920, O'Malley led a group of Volunteers that captured the RIC barracks in Ballytrain, County Monaghan, the first such success in Ulster. He worked closely with GHQ in organisation and training, which meant that he was close to Collins over many months. Likewise, he had a distinguished record in the field: he was involved in successful attacks on RIC barracks across Counties Kilkenny and Tipperary in May, June and July 1920. These latter engagements, which brought him into contact with Breen and Treacy – never far from any activity in those parts – required a degree of local initiative that placed them beyond central direction, although not central approval.

The British had one problem that they never resolved. Had Ireland been a distant crown colony in open rebellion, the matter would have been simple. Send the army in and let them sort it out. Ireland, however, was not a crown colony – although in its system of governance it was uncomfortably close to one – but rather a fully integrated part of the metropolitan United Kingdom. That this was a constitutional fiction was being made clearer by the day, but psychologically it inhibited Lloyd George from doing the one thing that might have worked.

After all, Collins never had more than 4,000 Volunteers at his disposal and not all of them were active simultaneously. The British Army could have flooded the country with troops but, as the politicians in London and as the new, reformed British administration in Dublin Castle knew even better, there was no purely military solution. Sooner or later, there would have to be some sort of political accommodation. The British had belatedly cleaned out the Augean Stable at the Castle and reformed it along best modern Treasury lines – ironically, just in time to hand it over to an independent Irish state in 1922. One of the clever young men in this new administration, Mark Grant Sturgis, sketched out the bones of a political solution in early 1920, just as the military campaign was escalating, and it proved to be remarkably prescient. Even as the sound of gunfire grew louder, the endgame was visible to those who had the head and the stomach for it.

In the meantime, it was mainly the guns that mattered. As early as February, Dublin was subject to a nightly curfew. Relations between IRA HQ in Dublin and Volunteer units in the provinces had stabilised to the point that some overall strategic direction was now viable. As early as New Year's Day, three barracks in the Cork area were attacked, with the full authority and encouragement of HQ. There were similar attacks elsewhere, mainly in the south and east, and some areas were placed under martial law.

On 15 January 1920, local government elections were held. It was the first time in Ireland that a system of proportional representation (PR) was employed and it did its job, nowhere more dramatically than in the city of Derry where the Catholic majority was allowed to count electorally for the first time and the old Unionist gerrymander – which depended on the first-past-the-post system – was overturned. When things calmed down a few years later, PR was abolished by the new devolved parliament in Belfast and it was back to business as usual for the next 40-odd years.

The aftermath of the burning of Cork city centre.

On 20 March 1920, his 36th birthday, Tomás MacCurtain was shot dead in front of his wife and son by a group of men with their faces disguised.

But it was at the other end of Ireland that the local elections produced results that woul resonate. The Cork IRA was divided into thr brigades. Tomás MacCurtain, officer-in-comm of the no. 1 city brigade, was not just elected Cork Corporation: he was elected lord mayor of the city, the first republican ever to hold th position. This was the same MacCurtain who led the New Year's Day attacks on the barrack His deputy was Terence MacSwiney.

Overall, Sinn Féin and associated parties controlled 172 out of 206 borough and urban district councils. This in effect meant their to domination once unionist Ulster is excluded. was a ringing endorsement of the result of the general election two months earlier, and it wa repeated and amplified in June when elections county councils and other local bodies, condu again under PR, produced similar results. Even in Ulster, Sinn Féin now controlle

35 of the 66 rural district councils, reflecting nationalist numbers west of the Bann.

On the evening of 20 March, a policeman was shot dead in Cork. In response, the area around Tomás MacCurtain's house was cordoned off; a group of men, their faces disguised, broke into the house and shot the lord mayor dead in front of his wife. The death of the policeman was soon forgotten; that of MacCurtain was not, and was to have consequences.

On 26 March, Collins's Squad struck once again in Dublin, shooting dead a magistrate, Alan Bell. Bell had been tasked by the British with investigating the sources of republican funds and confiscating them. It appears that he had done all too good a job, confiscating over £71,000 from Sinn Féin HQ. By trawling through bank accounts all over the country, he was on the way to seizing even more. He was a clear danger to the entire revolutionary enterprise. He was pulled off a tram in south Dublin and shot three times in the head. It was yet another case of Collins knowing that a dead man can be replaced, but the knowledge he carried in his head cannot.

There were changes in the British administration in Ireland in March 1920, around the time the Black and Tans were making their first appearance. Sir John Anderson, a brilliant young civil servant – he had already been chief civil servant in the Ministry of Shipping at the tender age of 34 – was sent across to oversee administration in Dublin Castle. One of his assistants was an extraordinary man called Alfred Cope, known to one and all as Andy. He had been a customs detective in the Ministry of Pensions. Somehow, Lloyd George got to know of him and took a shine to him. One maverick recognised another, perhaps. At any rate, Cope, now promoted to assistant under-secretary in the Irish administration, was able to open a back channel to Collins.

The new chief secretary was Canadian Sir Hamar Greenwood, a perfectly shameless liar. The new commander-in-chief of the army in Ireland was General Sir Nevil Macready, a man who had had a good war but who made no attempt to disguise his dislike of Ireland and the Irish. Overall, the British had improved the quality of the people in its Irish administration, especially in Dublin Castle, which they finally straightened out, while letting slip some very rough dogs of war in the shape of the Black and Tans.

The Tans soon showed what they were made of. On 27 April, a local IRA unit attacked the RIC barracks at Ballylanders, County Limerick, to the south-east of Limerick city and close to the county borders with Tipperary and Cork. This was already establishing itself as classic republican country. But this time the response was different. The Tans ignored Ballylanders, a tiny place of little consequence, but the night after the raid they shot up the centre of Limerick city, beginning a doleful tradition of terrorising civilians with complete indifference.

The war was now effectively being fought on two fronts. On the military side, the IRA flying columns, often consisting of small

Boy boarding up a window in Templemore in the aftermath of a raid by the Black and Tans.

numbers of men, prosecuted a war of movement and ambush in the countryside. Dublin, which was drenched with British security forces, saw little action until relatively late in the day. In parallel to all this, there was the intelligence war, directed by Collins in a manner that impressed – indeed, astonished – all contemporaries. Not only did he hobble the British intelligence system in Ireland, he had people in England who could give him reliable information on senior figures in the British security apparatus, up to and including Basil Thomson, the head of the Criminal Investigation Department.

Collins was unsentimental about dispatching double agents and spies. In one instance, a key associate of his, Liam Tobin from Cork, discovered a double agent and simply said to Collins that it would be necessary to shoot the man. 'We'll shoot him so', was Collins's immediate reply. And so it was done. The man was shot dead in a Dublin city centre street the following day. This was just one case of many. From the moment when Ned Broy had shown him how the British security system in Ireland worked, Collins drew the only logical conclusion. The British system was fatal to all Irish separatist ambitions and always had been in the past, and therefore it had to be dismantled. That meant killing people, and Collins did not hesitate to have them killed.

The fact that he had so many reliable informants within the police forces, especially the DMP, was evidence of the fragility of the British hold on Ireland. These were policemen, most often conservative and almost by instinct committed to the forces of order. Yet they were also Irish, and for many of them loyalty to nation and tribe overrode every other consideration. In a sense, the intelligence war was a coda to the 1918 conscription crisis: once nationalist Ireland flatly refused to fight in Britain's existential war, it was effectively voting itself out of the United Kingdom. For the policemen who were now supplying Michael Collins with inside information, this represented a change of loyalty that was transformative.

Again, it came down to legitimacy. The British hold on Ireland had progressively weakened decade on decade since the Famine. The Easter Rising and the

First World War British Army recruitment poster.

conscription crisis were accelerants in this process. It made it possible for Irish people from a broadly nationalist background – that included Collins's police informants – to transfer their personal loyalty to a new source of legitimacy. If that meant a betrayal of the old order, so be it. If it marked some men for certain death, so be it. Everyone in the War of Independence from Collins down lived dangerously. Any day might have been their last. He himself was the most wanted man in Ireland.

One incident in June 1920 was especially dramatic, and it stood symbolically for others. Lieutenant Colonel Bruce Smyth, a native of Banbridge, County Down, was now divisional commissioner of the RIC in Munster. In view of the security situation in Munster generally, it was proposed to make over some RIC barracks to the military. One such was in Listowel, County Kerry. Smyth addressed the collected policemen in the most incendiary terms, including the fateful words that 'the more you shoot the better I shall like you'. He made it plain that the policy was now ruthless war to the knife against Sinn Féin and the IRA, including the deployment of Black and Tans. The men refused. Their chosen spokesman, Jeremiah Mee, a 31-year-old constable from County Galway, stepped forward, removed his cap, belt and arms and resigned on the spot. So did a number of his colleagues.

Smyth ordered the immediate arrest of the mutineers. He was immediately warned off by the other men – those who were not resigning their commissions – who threatened violence if anyone laid a hand on Mee or anyone else. A month later, in Cork, the IRA killed Smyth.

Jeremiah Mee.

Lieutenant Colonel
Bruce Smyth.

District Inspector Oswald Swanzy.

Cork was a hotbed of rebellion. The city was seething in the wake of the murder of Tomás MacCurtain in February. An inquest jury had declared bluntly that 'the murder was organised and carried out by the RIC officially directed by the British government'. It returned a verdict of wilful murder against Lloyd George, Viceroy French, Chief Secretary Macpherson and District Inspector Oswald Swanzy of the RIC. Swanzy was quickly identified as the chief organiser of the murder and was spirited out of Cork to the safer pastures of Lisburn, County Antrim, just outside Belfast, a solidly unionist area. None the less, Collins's men caught up with him. Collins himself had been deeply affected by MacCurtain's killing and vowed revenge.

On 22 August – ironically, exactly two years to the day before Collins's own death – Swanzy was shot dead while leaving church in central Lisburn. The assassins were Cork IRA men who had travelled north, depending on local IRA units to 'finger' Swanzy. Sean Culhane, who had been one of Bruce Smyth's killers, was also one of those who fired on Swanzy: he used MacCurtain's personal revolver for the purpose. They then made good their escape south by travelling first class on the Dublin train, the authorities not supposing that assassins would travel in such style.

As the autumn came on, it seemed as if Ireland was descending into anarchy. Six RIC constables were shot in an IRA ambush in Macroom, County Cork, on 23 August. Sectarian rioting broke out in Belfast; east Ulster was to be convulsed by violence, in which Collins played no small part, for most of the next two years. The civil war that had been averted by the outbreak of the First World War six years earlier now took fire in the Ulster cockpit. On 20 September, a brawl in a pub near the small town of Balbriggan, just north of Dublin, resulted in gunshot wounds to two members of the Black and Tans, who had a camp nearby. The result was that the Tans did what they did best: they went on a rampage that left the centre of Balbriggan burned out. Two people died.

There were similar reprisals for ambushes and attacks in County Clare and, yet again, in County Cork. In the north of

The shooting of Seán
Treacy on Talbot Street,
Dublin, 14 October 1920.

that county, the military barracks at Mallow was captured by an IRA unit under Liam Lynch and Ernie O'Malley – the only such outright capture in the war – resulting in the sacking of the town by the military the following evening. And so it went on. Sean Treacy, originally of the South Tipperary brigade, died in a gunfight in Dublin. On 25 October, Terence MacSwiney, MacCurtain's successor as lord mayor of Cork, died on hunger strike in Brixton jail in London after 74 days without food. On 1 November, Kevin Barry, aged 18, was hanged in Mountjoy jail in Dublin; the gunfight he had been involved in on 20 September had also accounted for the life of a 15-year-old British squaddie.

In early November, an IRA unit under Seán Mac Eoin held the town of Ballinalee, County Longford, for five days before the British could recapture it. In gratitude, they set it alight. Then came what was beyond question the most fateful day in Michael Collins's career as a military planner: 21 November, Bloody Sunday. The story has been told and retold and only the bare bones require summary here. In the morning, Collins dispatched the Squad to kill 14 alleged British agents. Many were shot in their beds; some were innocent, although there is no doubt about the culpability of others. The British had stepped up their intelligence operation in Dublin and were getting uncomfortably close to

Collins himself. Three of his closest associates, Frank Thornton, Tom Cullen and Liam Tobin, were all 'lifted' and interrogated. Collins decided to strike before he was struck: thus the killings on the morning of Bloody Sunday.

In the afternoon and evening came the reprisals. In Dublin Castle, three prisoners – Dick McKee, Peadar Clancy and Conor Clune – were executed in cold blood by the Auxiliaries. McKee and Clancy were senior IRA men; poor Clune, while a nationalist, was only in Dublin on business and was just unlucky, a case of being in the wrong place at the wrong time. Earlier, 11 spectators and one player died when the police – a mixture of regular RIC men, Tans and Auxiliaries – fired into a crowd at a Gaelic football match in Croke Park, the headquarters of the GAA in north Dublin.

In December, an IRA ambush on the RIC's Victoria barracks in Cork produced a reprisal from the Black and Tans that left the city centre burned out. One measure of how effective the IRA's war campaign had been was supplied to parliament in London by the Foreign Secretary, Lord Curzon. He reported on the results of IRA activity from 1 January 1919 to 18 October 1920. This had seen 64 courthouses destroyed; 492 RIC barracks destroyed; a further 114 damaged and vacated; 21 barracks occupied by the RIC destroyed and a further 48 damaged; 741 raids on the postal service; 40 raids on coastguard stations and lighthouses; 117 policemen dead and 185 injured; 23 military dead and 71 wounded; 32 civilians killed and 83 wounded; 148 private residences destroyed, all of them belonging to unionists.

It was a melancholy inventory and the war dragged on for another nine months after that. But Curzon's catalogue was a testament to the effectiveness of the campaign directed by Collins. Add in the single-minded disabling of the British intelligence apparatus in Ireland – for which the credit goes to Collins alone – and one can get some measure of the central importance of this exceptional man, not yet 30, to the entire effort to rid Ireland of British rule. He was simply referred to as the Big Fellow.

At this point, on 23 December 1920, the Long Fellow returned. Éamon de Valera had spent the previous 18 months in the United States, raising funds for the Irish cause and spreading the word in support of Irish separatism. It had been a bumpy ride, because there were factions in the higher reaches of Irish-American life, which meant poisoned rivalries and divided counsels. De Valera earnestly wished to steer clear of these internal divisions but could not. They weakened the potential effect of his tour without fatally damaging it. Irish-America was in no doubt that it stood four-square behind the Irish republic, and the dollars flowed.

The Ireland to which de Valera returned was a very different place from the one he had left in the summer of 1919. Back then, the War of Independence had barely got going. When he returned it was at full throttle. Moreover, Collins had moved from being a major figure in the revolutionary firmament to being absolutely central to it. De Valera was the President of Dáil Éireann and had not scrupled to style himself President of the Irish Republic while in the United States. It was an appellation that few Irish nationalists would deny him. Even in the higher ranks of the IRA, there was occasional resentment at Collins's habit of belittling de Valera's ignorance of or naivety concerning military affairs. De Valera was, after all, the political leader of the nation and entitled to the deference due to his position. It was unreasonable to expect him to be across every military detail. Here was the germ of future difficulties. Collins may have been the Big Fellow, but a lot of senior people in the movement did not like him or his style, or his hectoring and bullying, or his maddening efficiency and insistence on punctuality.

On the very day that de Valera stepped off the boat from America, Ireland was partitioned. Given all that had happened since 1912, the Third Home Rule Act was a dead letter. Westminster passed what was in effect a fourth Home Rule bill, the Government of Ireland Act 1920, which became law on 23 December. It proposed two parliaments, one in Belfast for a new six-county entity to be known henceforth as Northern Ireland, and the other in Dublin to govern what would be known as Southern Ireland.

Collins's own interpretation of partition, which he felt like a wound, was typical of the confusion of mind and wilful avoidance of hard sectarian realities that has characterised Irish nationalists since O'Connell. For Collins, it was all part of a British grand plan, rather than a despairing expedient. Like most nationalists, Collins could not accept what was the unwelcome truth: that Ulster unionists did not and could not by definition give any allegiance, rational or emotional, to Irish nationalism. Yet Collins regarded them as a part of the Irish nation that was being conveniently used by Britain for her own nefarious imperial purposes.

'The [partition] act entrenched [the Orange leaders] (or appeared to) within the six counties. No doubt, both the British and Orange leaders had it in mind that if a bigger settlement had ultimately to be made with Ireland, a position was secured from which they could bargain.

'In any settlement the North-East was to be let down gently by the British government. Pampered for so long they had learned to dictate to and to bully the nation to which they professed to be loyal. They must be treated with tact in regard to any change of British policy towards Ireland ... .

'North-East Ulster had been created and maintained not for her own advantage, but to uphold Britain's policy. Everything was done to divide the Irish people and to keep them apart. If we could be made to believe we were the enemies of each other, the real enemy would be overlooked. In this policy Britain has been completely successful. She petted a minority into becoming her agents with the double advantage of maintaining her policy and keeping us divided.'

In short, Collins's desolate analysis of the North was a mixture of unsupported assertions, despair in the face of uncomfortable facts on the ground and an automatic attribution of bad faith to

Britain: the standard nationalist boilerplate. Here was the one great issue where the supreme realist could not bear to face reality.

Collins did everything he could to strangle Northern Ireland at birth, as we shall see. It hardly amounted to 'treating them with tact'. There was already in place a boycott of goods sourced in Belfast, a rather feeble gesture that achieved next to nothing and was abandoned when convenient. The real military effort in the north had to await cessation of hostilities in the south. That did not happen until July 1921. Before that, there were notable guerrilla actions, especially in West Cork at Kilmichael and Crossbarry, where the Cork no. 3 brigade of the IRA inflicted defeats on British forces. Another lord mayor, George Clancy of Limerick, was assassinated. He had been a college contemporary and friend of James Joyce; indeed Joyce had modelled the character of Davin in

IRA volunteers cook breakfast, Old Parish area, Waterford, during the Civil War c. 1922.

181

A Portrait of the Artist as a Young Man on him.

Gradually, tensions arose between de Valera and Collins. De Valera was very conscious of his status as president, and was set on asserting his authority. He did so by making Austin Stack, a Kerry man of limited ability, president-designate, the position that Collins had held while de Valera was in America. That was one thing. Quite another was that de Valera had a view of military strategy that was different from that of Collins, which inevitably irritated Collins, whose methods had achieved so much in so little time and with such slender resources. But de Valera was political to his fingertips

Éamon de Valera.

and he wanted actions that had public relations value. For the most part, Collins was able to hold the line against de Valera, but the one instance in which he failed to do this was to prove an embarrassing fiasco.

This was the burning of the Custom House in Dublin in May 1921. It was – and still is, in its restored condition – the finest classical building in the city. It was also the centre of the British local government bureaucracy, holding sensitive files and tax records. An IRA raiding party torched the building but then found themselves trapped inside as the British response was almost instantaneous. Six Volunteers died in the subsequent shooting, while twelve were wounded. Between 70 and 130 were captured. De Valera got his public relations coup but Collins was furious. His temper was not improved when the Squad and the entire intelligence operation were folded into the Dublin Brigade of the IRA, removing them from Collins's direct influence and bringing them formally under the command of de Valera and Cathal Brugha, the minister of defence, whose dislike of Collins was growing by the day.

By any calculation, the burning of the Custom House was a military disaster for the IRA, the worst of the entire conflict. It had been no accident that Dublin had been relatively quiet in the war, given the huge British military presence. The IRA, as directed by Collins, had conducted a series of hit-and-run ambushes in the countryside. Their units were not well armed, so they had to have the advantage of surprise and the speed to get away fast after the action. This was not an army set up for the sort of static warfare that de Valera desired, and the Custom House fiasco was proof of it. It greatly weakened the republican war effort and hurried the advance towards a cessation of hostilities.

Collins was also feeling the heat from the British side. Their intelligence operation was improving; they discovered the location of the home affairs department and even raided Collins's own office, although fortunately he was not there at the time. As he wrote: 'They just walked into the office where they expected to find me working. The information was good and I ought to have been there at the time … . It was the most providential escape yet.' It was clear that Collins's fabled luck could not hold forever. Ned Broy had been arrested in December 1920 after documents prepared by him were found in the house of a Sinn Féin sympathiser.

By the summer of 1921 there was a series of moves which,

when aggregated, pointed towards a truce. King George V opened the new Northern Ireland parliament in Belfast and made a conciliatory speech. Andy Cope, who was closer to Collins than any other British official and who favoured a policy of conciliation – in sharp contrast to the malevolent chief secretary, Greenwood – was summoned to address a full cabinet meeting in London on what he knew and how he assessed things. Mark Grant Sturgis in Dublin Castle also opened up back-channel contacts to influential figures in Irish nationalist life, especially in the labour movement. A key back channel was that opened between Jan Smuts, prime minister of South Africa, who was in London for an imperial conference, and de Valera. Smuts had Lloyd George's ear.

There was a near glitch on 22 June – the same day that King George was speaking in Belfast – when de Valera was briefly arrested in Dublin but was quickly released on the authority of the ubiquitous Andy Cope. De Valera and Arthur Griffith then had meetings with Lord Midleton, representing the interests of the increasingly beleaguered southern unionists, but who agreed to act as an intermediary with Lloyd George. The upshot was a cessation of hostilities announced for noon on 11 July, on the basis of headline terms negotiated by the British military and representatives of Sinn Féin.

CHAPTER 9

Treaty

'I tell you
this, early this
morning I have
signed my own
death warrant.'

Michael Collins

The truce in the south contrasted dramatically with the renewed outbreak of sectarian violence in the newborn Northern Ireland. Ulster was a tinder box: partition and the creation of Northern Ireland left the nationalist minority trapped within its borders feeling abandoned. In the south, de Valera placed greater emphasis on projecting the principle of republicanism than on condemning partition. That is not to say that de Valera was indifferent to partition – far from it, he considered it a moral and political abomination – but in 1921 and 1922 his greater emphasis was on trying to secure a settlement with Britain that could be represented as substantially republican.

With Collins, the emphasis was otherwise. Although a republican, he realised that Lloyd George would never concede a republic, if only because he could not concede a republic: he may have been a Liberal, but he had split his party; now his government was a coalition dominated by Conservatives. For Collins, however, partition was a primal wound. He felt it viscerally. Moreover, he felt in a position to do something about it. The truce in the south freed up IRA Volunteers to go north.

The north was chronically unstable at the best of times, but a full outbreak of hostilities between Protestants and Catholics

began in April 1920 in Derry, following
the election there of the city's first-ever
Catholic mayor. By June, the death toll was
40 and the British army were deployed to
keep the two sides apart, which they did
by allying themselves with the local UVF.
In July Protestant workers in the Belfast
shipyards drove out Catholic workers,
accompanied by the traditional helping of
'Belfast confetti' – rivets. Some men had to
jump into Belfast Lough and swim for their
lives. Passions were inflamed: it was the day
of the funeral of Colonel Bruce Smyth from
Banbridge, who had been shot by the IRA
in Cork. The killing of Swanzy in Lisburn
followed hard on this, leaving the Catholic
minority in Belfast and its environs in a
perilous position.

They had little with which to defend
themselves and their property, and they
were now faced by an opposition that had
the entire resources of the new statelet

The funeral of Colonel
Smyth at Victoria
Barracks, Cork, 1920.

behind them. These were the circumstances in which Collins sent IRA Volunteers from the south up north, at least to stiffen nationalist resistance to sectarian attack and to try to equalise the situation. He also hoped to make the new Northern Ireland unviable, both by destabilising it militarily and by promoting policies in Dublin that would cause maximum economic damage in the North.

The next two years – until the early summer of 1922 – was a time of hopeless, futile, sectarian viciousness in north-east Ulster. The death toll was 557, of whom 303 were Catholics and 172 were Protestants, all civilians. In addition, 82 members of the security forces died. Then there were the injuries, the social humiliations, the destruction of property and the loss of businesses – and the abandonment of any hope that a normal civil society might take root. Collins's reinforcement of the nationalist muscle, already pretty feeble, may have been a futile gesture. But it may also have saved the nationalist community from even greater losses. What it did not do was what Collins had most earnestly desired: to destroy Northern Ireland at birth. There would be other days.

Three days after the truce took hold, de Valera went to London to see Lloyd George. They had three exploratory meetings at which there was no real meeting of minds. De Valera engaged in what was soon to become a standard routine, by offering a summary of Irish history at a length designed to confuse, if not anaesthetise, his interlocutor. Lloyd George made it clear that a republic was out of the question; de Valera refused to accept dominion home rule, which was on offer. In this refusal, he had the support of the Sinn Féin cabinet back in Dublin. There was no common ground on which these two subtle, calculating and supremely political minds could meet.

This failure set the agenda for what followed in the next few months until the conclusion

Talks in London 1921 between Lloyd George and de Valera.

'We have to
learn that
freedom imposes
responsibilities.'

Michael Collins

Sir James Craig.

of the Anglo-Irish treaty in December. As
Collins was to make clear more than once,
the republic was never on the table. But
partition just might be, if Ulster could be
coerced: there is little doubt that the British
would have coerced Ulster if they could
have got away with it. But Sir James Craig,
now prime minister of Northern Ireland,
dug his heels in and refused to give an inch,
an attitude that became a default setting for
his tribe thereafter.

If Craig wouldn't budge, Lloyd
George was out of options. For political
reasons he couldn't possibly concede a
republic, or anything like it. As he stated
in writing: 'The British government could
not acknowledge the right of Ireland to
secede from allegiance to her king.' This
was transparently false; his majesty was
in no sense Ireland's king, other than in
constitutional fiction, as nationalist Ireland
had demonstrated so eloquently during

the 1918 conscription crisis by declining to fight for him when he was up against it. But there was always the possibility of fudging the border in some way, potentially to buy off the other source of nationalist grievance. That is roughly how the thing played out.

There followed some weeks of back-and-forthing between London and Dublin, with an exchange of forms of words designed to be as delicate as porcelain. Towards the end of September, Lloyd George came up with the Gairloch formula, proposing that British and Irish delegates should meet 'with a view to ascertaining how the association of nations known as the British Empire may best be reconciled with Irish national aspirations'. This formula was accepted in Dublin. The Dáil had already approved the appointment of Irish delegates in this pursuit. They were Arthur Griffith, Michael Collins, George Gavan Duffy, Robert Childers Barton and Eamonn Duggan. Duggan was a lawyer who was influential in Sinn Féin and had accompanied de Valera to the July talks with Lloyd George in London. In general, he followed the line in the discussions supported by Griffith and Collins. Duffy was another lawyer, the son of a Young Irelander of the 1840s and therefore of impeccable pedigree, whose support for the eventual treaty was, on his own account, a rational calculation even though his emotion was pulling him to the other side. Barton was a gent, educated at Rugby and heir to more than 1,500 acres of land in County Wicklow. His cousin Erskine Childers, to whom he was extremely close, was appointed secretary to the delegation.

These were the minor players. No one was in any doubt about two things. First, Griffith and Collins were the men of substance and they would provide the leadership on the Irish side. The second was the startling absence of the leader of the Irish nation, Éamon de Valera, acknowledged as the outstanding political intellect in Ireland and a negotiator of sufficient sophistication to get under the skin and exasperate even as gifted a conjuror as Lloyd George. There is much to be said for that ability, and the delegation appointed did not have it; they had left behind in Dublin the one indispensable man who, on any rational reckoning, should not simply have been on the delegation but should have been leading it.

It is one of the great what-ifs of Irish history. Why didn't de Valera go to London? There have been many theories; this is hardly the place to summarise them or to add to them. But he did not – which left Griffith and Collins in the spotlight. The conference began on 11 October and concluded on 6 December with the signing of the treaty.

The Irish negotiating team, without Collins, departing for the treaty talks in London, October 1921.

Collins was the star item on the Irish side. Up until now, he was known only as a ruthless fighting man who generated much understandable hatred on the British side, but also a surprising degree of frank admiration. More than one senior British figure could scarce forbear to cheer – how they could have done with someone like him on their side – but he had remained until now something of a man of mystery, that scarlet pimpernel that no amount of British intelligence could lay a hand on. And now here he was, in the heart of the imperial metropolis: handsome, well-

dressed, self-possessed. He was anyone's idea of a young hero, a Napoleonic general, perhaps, and not at all like anyone's idea of a common murderer. The British were not an imperial people for nothing. They knew a good one when they saw him, and many of them – especially Birkenhead and Churchill, of all improbable people – came to like, admire and befriend him. Some people have star quality, and often – sadly – it is enhanced by a capacity for violence. Collins had it, and the British knew he had it.

By now, the autumn of 1921, it was three and a half years since Collins had first lodged in the Greville Arms Hotel in Longford and fallen in love with Kitty Kiernan, the sister of the proprietor. His close colleague, Harry Boland, had also fallen madly in love with Kitty. All three knew the reality of this triangle, hardly an unprecedented occurrence in human affairs but one obviously freighted with the potential for tragedy, which was in the course of time realised in full.

Collins did not sail to London with the other delegates. He had an important matter to settle in Dublin: an informal betrothal 'arrangement' with Kitty Kiernan. It seems clear that they had reached some understanding in early October but no formal announcement of their engagement was made until March 1922.

The love of Michael Collins's life, Kitty Kiernan.

We are fortunate to have a selection of the letters that were exchanged by Michael and Kitty, edited and annotated by the late León Ó Broin. The earliest is undated, but Ó Broin estimates it to be February or March 1919, or nearly two years after Collins had first lodged in Granard. The salutation is 'My darling Kitty', which Ó Broin thinks is used casually rather than passionately, adding that 'it would be mid-summer of 1921 before Collins would speak to Kitty in the terms of deep affection which the word can imply'. I think that this is a fair judgement, although one remains conscious that this was a more formal age than ours and that such a salutation – or 'love' in valediction – potentially carried a register of greater weight than it might today.

There is no evidence of a firm commitment by both until October, when Collins assures Kitty, 'You are the one – never fear'. By October 1921 Collins was sufficiently committed to enter into the 'arrangement'. In his last letter to Kitty before leaving for London, written in the Gresham Hotel, Dublin, on 9 October, he says simply: 'I feel today that arrangements of ours may be made more binding – do you think so?'

This is tepid stuff compared to Harry Boland's letters to Kitty around this time. He was in the United States with de Valera and was clearly a man madly in love and unaware that his friend Collins was as far advanced in Kitty's affections as he clearly was. It was messy, to put it mildly. On 1 October – just a week before Collins and Kitty made their 'arrangement', Boland wrote to Kitty from Cork immediately before setting sail for the United States. His salutation was 'Pulse of my heart' and the key passage of the letter was this:

'How I can leave you even at the order of "the Chief" I do not know, and I'm asking myself all the time if I haven't made a great mistake in leaving you behind. Won't you send me a wireless to the Celtic to say you have made up your mind? If you have done so, cable Yes, and if you are still in doubt, then for God's sake try to make up your mind, and agree to come with me.' Almost tragically, he added that 'Mick [Collins] and I spent the last night together.' He then signs off by writing: 'I

Harry Boland.

bid you a fond farewell and, as I can not kiss you with my lips, I do so a million times with the lips of my heart. May God bless and guard you. Your devoted lover, Harry.'

What Harry Boland was proposing to Kitty Kiernan in that letter was an outright proposal of marriage. As if now to turn tragedy to farce, he seems to have believed his proposal accepted – although we don't know if any cable, good or bad, was sent by Kitty. But, for whatever reason, Boland's mother believed that they had agreed to be married and wrote to Kitty on 4 October: 'As Harry tells me you are engaged to be married to him, allow me to congratulate you, and to wish every joy and blessing God can bestow on you both, for a better son never lived than Harry … .'

Boland was labouring under a tragic misapprehension. It is not entirely clear how he learned of Collins's success with Kitty, but it appears that Collins himself broke the news to him when he returned from the United States in December. It prompted the following note from Harry to Kitty, his salutatory cough now very much softened:

'Kitty, I want to congratulate you. M. told me of your engagement, and I wish you long life and happiness. Ever yours, H. Boland.'

So, in December, two months into Collins's 'arrangement' with Kitty, he is telling Boland that he is engaged to be married to her, although no public announcement to that effect was to be made for another three months. In the meantime, Collins had been at the treaty conference in London, with lurid rumours of his affairs with society women already circulating freely. None the less, there seems no doubt about Kitty's commitment, for as early as late October she is writing to him: 'You are never out of my heart.' She then sent a follow-up note, signing off with, 'I send you a big hug as well as a kiss with my love. Your own little pet … '. Her letter is undated but headed 'Wednesday' in reply to his note from London dated 21 October, a Friday. So Kitty's letter was probably written on the 26th.

Maddeningly, so many of her letters to him around this crucial time are undated, although the key letter is headed Thursday, which suggests the 27th. Towards the end, she blurts it out, plain as day: 'My hand is getting cold. I can't write, but I want you to know that I love you oh so much.' As the weeks and months pass, she remains ardent in her mode of address to him; he too to her, although less obviously effusive. Collins was a cautious man by nature, a rational calculator of odds. One of the considerations that must have crossed his mind was that his letters might be intercepted – he himself had intercepted enough letters in his career – by people who would look to put the worst possible construction on everything. But there is little to doubt his love for Kitty. He addresses her as 'my own dearest Kitty' and 'My own Kit', and the mere fact of the consistency and continuity of their correspondence, right to the end, tells its own tale.

The conference in London to settle Anglo-Irish affairs began at 11 o'clock on the morning of 11 October 1921. The Gairloch formula, which Lloyd George had crafted, established the terms of reference under which the talks would take place. There was

one word absent from the formula: republic. It was a concept that no British government of the day could have conceded. The fact that it was effectively conceded in later decades is neither here nor there: circumstances change and the world bends in time to new realities. But time is the critical factor. The republic may have been a perfectly wonderful idea – it was – but it was utterly unrealisable in the real world of 1921.

Collins grasped this better than de Valera. Collins was Supreme Head of the IRB, a Fenian through and through, but he was also a maker of trial balances and of balance sheets: finance Collins, whose psychology drove organisational Collins, efficient administrative Collins, punctual Collins. These were opposite ends of his personality pulling him in opposite directions. It was he, not de Valera, who demonstrated the greater political flexibility, the accommodation to reality. De Valera was regarded as supreme in this area, but it's hard not to think that a mixture of overweening vanity and an almost Jesuitical insistence on absolute purity drove him mad in these crucial years.

Lloyd George at first got it all wrong, marking Collins down as the sea-green irreconcilable – it was understandable: finance Collins had been well occluded from the Welsh Wizard's view –

A prayer vigil outside the Anglo-Irish Treaty negotiations in 1921, which marked the end of the Anglo-Irish War.

while regarding de Valera as the difficult, tedious but ultimately malleable man. That's not how the game played out at all. De Valera had had three meetings with Lloyd George in July, as we saw, and rational de Valera could hardly have emerged from these discussions other than knowing – and knowing well – that whatever was potentially on offer from the British, the republic was not. The Gairloch formula for the conference that actually took place confirmed this. Yet de Valera persisted in his republic fixation past the point of reason. Was he being irrational? If he was, he had lots of people who were willing to follow him over the cliff edge, which is exactly where they found themselves when the Civil War came.

Collins, on the other hand, the young political tyro, good for nothing in Lloyd George's eyes other than the sneakiest types of murder and ruthlessness (things,

'It gives us freedom, not the ultimate freedom … but the freedom to achieve it.'

Michael Collins

of course, of which the British Empire was completely innocent), read the situation with a shrewder eye, and an honest one. He immediately recognised that the Gairloch formula, which the Sinn Féin leadership had accepted as the basis for the conference – precluded the republic. 'If we all stood on the recognition of the Irish Republic as a prelude to any conference we could very easily have said so, and there would have been no conference … '. The terms of reference that underlay the conference logically proposed the compromise that emerged from it. If a 'gunman', not yet 30 years of age, could see this with such clarity, how could de Valera, supposedly the master logician, not?

Collins hadn't wanted to go to London as part of the Irish delegation. When he could not persuade de Valera to go and was obliged to go himself, he was blunt in telling de Valera that whatever the delegates might bring back from the talks, it would not be a republic. This was the head of the IRB explaining the facts of life to a realist temporarily turned fantasist. The Irish delegation was given plenipotentiary powers to conclude an agreement with Britain, were such an agreement possible, but subject to the condition that 'the complete text of the draft treaty about to be signed will be … submitted to Dublin, and a reply awaited'. So they were and were not plenipotentiaries at the same time.

In London, Collins became de facto leader of the Irish delegation. Griffith was barely 50 but he was ill and worn down by years of poverty. Years later, long after he was dead, Yeats contemplated his portrait in the Municipal Gallery in Dublin and wrote of 'Griffith staring in hysterical pride', which captured some of him but by no means all. He was prickly and he stood on his honour. Indeed, it was standing on his honour at the conference that was the hinge moment on which the whole thing was to turn, refusing to dishonour his word to that most dishonourable chancer, David Lloyd George.

But Griffith's ill health meant that in effect Collins became the lead Irish negotiator. This position was made more sensitive by the manner in which the conference avoided, as far as possible, plenary sessions in favour of sub-committee discussions between the principals. While Griffith remained the head of the Irish delegation, his position was something more than nominal but never dominant. Collins was obliged to do most of the heavy lifting. The British had formed a view that the other Irish delegates were of no great account – they were particularly dismissive of Robert Barton – and through their intelligence operation in Ireland, improving by the week, they had a reasonable handle on nationalist public opinion, and in particular on what that public opinion might be disposed to accept by way of compromise. All this found its way to Downing Street.

So Collins was up against a formidable diplomatic apparatus. Yet he never lost sight of the fact that the terms of reference of the conference pointed only towards compromise and something short of the republic. In that context, the job was to get the best deal possible in the circumstances. The British certainly out-manoeuvred the Irish in the negotiating endgame – Lloyd George shamelessly doing what he did best, out of terrible necessity – but that was tactical. Strategically, what Collins and the others brought back from London was as good a deal as could be secured in the real world. For a crowd of tyros and nonentities, they did very well indeed.

The hinge moment was this. On 2 November, Griffith had a bilateral meeting with Lloyd George. The prime minister had a political difficulty with the Conservative Party ultras who deplored the mere fact of the British government negotiating with Sinn Féin in the first place. In order to placate them, he got Griffith to sign a note to the effect that Ireland would remain associated with the crown 'in return for essential unity', but added that he would not collapse the talks over Northern Ireland. This was contrary to the entire negotiating strategy of the Irish side, which had resolved that if there were to be a break, it should be on the republic and not on Ulster.

Griffith apparently thought that he was merely helping Lloyd George out of a short-term political difficulty. But by signing the note – the wording of which had been the work of Tom Jones, the cabinet assistant secretary – he was potentially undermining his own side's negotiating position. The other Irish delegates had rejected an earlier draft and insisted that any note should be signed by all of them or none. So Griffith went very far out on a limb in signing unilaterally. Perhaps he thought it wise to give Lloyd George some political cover because he was at least a Liberal and the alternative would have been his replacement by the hardliner Andrew Bonar Law, the Tory party leader, who would probably have broken off the conference altogether. However, not only did Griffith sign the note unilaterally, he did not apprise his colleagues, including Collins, of it.

So, on the evening of 5 December in Downing Street, with the talks seemingly at an impasse, Lloyd George produced the letter like a rabbit out of a hat and flourished it. Collins declared that he had no idea what it was, only for Lloyd George to rub his nose in it by saying: 'Do you mean to tell me, Mr Collins, that you never learned of this document from Mr Griffith?' He then asked Griffith pointedly if he was now about to break faith and dishonour his own signature. This was the moment when Griffith's 'hysterical pride' kicked in. He said that he had never let anyone down in his life and he was not about to do so now.

Lloyd George had shown a lack of scruple and a political ruthlessness that was utterly typical of him. He was a power animal through and through. Griffith had no such power lust, was in poor health – he would be dead of a cerebral haemorrhage within the year – and had fallen for a trick. The treaty was duly signed in the early hours of the following morning after some theatrical threats of immediate war from Lloyd George, now well in command of the whole business. It is easy, at this remove, to forget just how formidable a man the Welsh Wizard was. Some years later, when he had retired and Churchill was now ascendant as chancellor of the exchequer, the two men met and, in Churchill's words, 'resumed our previous roles of master and pupil – and I was the pupil'.

The treaty created the Irish Free State as a self-governing dominion within the British Commonwealth; a boundary commission was to revisit the question of Northern Ireland territoriality at a later date. The republic that had never been on the table was not mentioned. Later, as he was returning to Ireland, Collins wrote, in a stirring piece of eloquence: 'Think – what have I got for Ireland? Something she has wanted these past seven hundred years. Will anyone be satisfied at the bargain? Will anyone? I tell you this – early this morning I signed my death warrant.'

Treaty talks in the cabinet room, 10 Downing Street, London, in 1921. *Left:* the British team including Lloyd George and Winston Churchill. *Right:* the heads of the Irish delegation, Michael Collins and Arthur Griffith.

'Lloyd George ... I find to be particularly obnoxious. He is all comradely, all craft and wiliness – all arm around the shoulder ... not long ago he would have had me joyfully at the rope end.'

Michael Collins

CHAPTER 10
Provisional Government

'There is
no British
Government
any longer
in Ireland. It
is gone. It is
no longer the
enemy.'

Michael Collins

The ratification of the Anglo-Irish Treaty, Mansion House, Dublin, January 1922.

The treaty was signed – but would the Dáil endorse it? The document signed in London had aroused passions in Ireland that would endure for generations, and the aftershocks are occasionally felt to this day. It quickly got personal. Collins was accused of the old slur – a favourite among Irish nationalist radicals – that he had been corrupted by the fleshpots of decadent London. There was a strong puritan streak in Irish nationalism, as in most revolutionary movements, and the pantomime image of the upright, moral provincial boy seduced and corrupted by the bright lights and perfumed women of the gaudy metropolis was too tempting to pass up.

Collins's name was associated with a number of women in the London beau monde, even including a member of the royal family. No hard evidence was produced in support of most of these fantasies, nor did they take account of the fact – which Collins himself acknowledged publicly – that Kitty Kiernan back in Ireland was already his intended. Collins was handsome and had the magnetic attraction of the dashing, revolutionary outsider now swaggering in the halls of the mighty, a real grand opera leading man. He was attractive to women, and there is no doubt that some women in London found him so: two claimed to have had an affair with him. But any suggestions of an affair or affairs

were supported by nothing more than these
assertions or by circumstantial evidence and
suggestive gossip and hearsay. He may have
had an affair or affairs; 'arrangements' and
engagements, or indeed marriages, haven't
stopped anyone yet. The point is that we
don't know now and they didn't know
then. None of which stopped the wild
accusations of the 'hard man' corrupted
by the sinful city and its loose women.
This prurient tittle-tattle provided some of
the background to the Treaty debates and
helped to account for some of the lingering
bitterness that they engendered.

It was already clear that the Sinn Féin
cabinet was badly divided on the terms of
the treaty. On first learning of its contents
de Valera immediately indicated his
opposition; his prestige and influence alone
ensured that political opinion would be
divided, although that degree of division
was never reflected to the same extent

Éamon de Valera, 1920.

among the wider nationalist press and public, which were generally supportive of the deal. A cabinet meeting in early December had supported the treaty by a mere four votes to three, with de Valera, Austin Stack and Cathal Brugha in the minority.

De Valera immediately issued a public statement in strident opposition to the treaty, which set the tone for much of the tragedy that was to follow. He claimed that its terms were 'in violent conflict with the wishes of the majority of this nation'. This was not obvious to the citizens of the nation, whose reception for the treaty was enthusiastic; this was demonstrated spontaneously at the time and would be confirmed electorally within six months.

As to the debates themselves, they began formally on 14 December 1921. The pro- and anti-treaty principals sat opposite

Michael Collins's arrival back in Ireland after the negotiations.

each other, for all the world like a government and opposition in a mini-House of Commons. In adopting that configuration, each side set out its stall. Most of the proceedings were predictable and only the contributions of the principals are germane to this book, because they stated the case for and against the treaty in a manner that merely invited repetition by their subordinates.

De Valera, as president of the Dáil, opened. His key point was that the delegates in London had exceeded their powers by signing the treaty without further reference back to Dublin for approval or otherwise. At the same time, he allowed that the delegates had been granted plenipotentiary powers. These positions were mutually incompatible, as was quickly pointed out. He continued to offer his counter-proposal, known as Document No. 2, which required no oath of allegiance and would merely have associated an independent Ireland with the empire while remaining outside any formal membership of it. It was a perfectly sensible proposal, subtle and clever, and it certainly reflected the reality of Irish nationalist expectations. It was later – in the 1930s – adopted in substance. But in late 1921 it was premature and the British were never going to accept it: they had already rejected out of hand a version of it tabled during the treaty negotiations.

Collins was conflicted. He was a militant and sincere republican, the director of the IRA's war effort and the head of the IRB. But he also was developing a more sensitive understanding of the realities of power. Whatever Michael Collins was or wasn't, he was a realist first and last. His realism – combined with his ruthlessness – had brought nationalist Ireland this far, further than she could have dreamed of 10 years earlier. The treaty, as it stood, represented a considerable advance on the suspended (and now redundant) Home Rule Act. Whether the gains it represented were worth the expenditure of lives, property and human decency during the revolutionary years is a matter for moralists. But it was an advance.

Collins's case to the Dáil was basically that this was as much as could realistically be achieved for the moment. Moreover, he knew better than anyone that in July, at the time of the truce, the IRA was in a bad way and incapable of maintaining its offensive capacity for much longer. The truce saved the IRA from military defeat and provided the context for the treaty. Seán Mac Eoin, the hero of Ballinalee, calculated that the IRA comprised no more than 4,000 Volunteers, with no more than one rifle for every 50 men. Collins knew this better than anyone. If the army could not fight its way to outright victory, it might have to settle for the best that could be got. As he had said to Barton, the most reluctant signatory of the treaty in London: 'Do you want me to send them out to be slaughtered?' De Valera had declared that it was better to go back to war than renege on the republic. Collins, who understood the military realities – as de Valera had repeatedly proved incapable of doing – was not prepared to do so.

Collins's key statement in the debate on the treaty was this:

'In my opinion it gives us freedom, not the ultimate freedom that all nations desire and develop to, but the freedom to achieve it.'

Both in the Dáil debate and elsewhere, he elaborated on some of the key considerations behind the acceptance of the treaty.

'We had not … succeeded in getting the government entirely into our own hands, and we had not succeeded in beating the British out of Ireland, militarily.

'We had unquestionably seriously interfered with their government, and we had prevented them from conquering us. That was the sum of our achievement. We had reached in July the high-water mark of what we could do in the way of economic and military resistance …

'We had recognised our inability to beat the British out of Ireland, and we recognised what that inability meant. Writing in the weekly called *The Republic of Ireland* on 21 February last, Mr Barton, a former member of the Dáil cabinet, stated that before the truce of 11 July it "had become plain that it was physically impossible to secure Ireland's ideal of a completely isolated republic otherwise than by driving the overwhelmingly superior British forces out of the country".'

He now belatedly began to accept northern realities. 'We [the treaty delegates] also recognised facts in regard to north-east Ulster. We clearly recognised that our national view was not shared by the majority in the four north-eastern counties. We knew that the majority had refused to give allegiance to an Irish republic. Before we entered the conference, we realised these facts among ourselves. We had abandoned, for the time being, the hope of achieving the ideal of achieving independence under the republican form.'

Amid all the pressure of the treaty discussions in London, Collins had taken the trouble to acquaint himself with the nature of dominion status, by reading the works of various academic authorities on the subject. He had satisfied himself that not only was it the best offer Sinn Féin was likely to secure, it was the only practical means of squaring the circle.

'Sir Robert Borden, in the peace treaty debate in the Canadian House on 2 September 1919, claimed for Canada "a complete sovereignty". This claim has never been challenged by Britain.' He then pointed out that Smuts had made a similar unchallenged claim for South Africa, adding: 'In other words, the former dependent dominions of the British Commonwealth are now free and secure in their freedom. That position of freedom, and of freedom from interference, we have secured in the treaty … . Our status in association with the British nations would be the constitutional status of Canada. The definition of that status is the bedrock of the treaty. It is the recognition of our right to freedom, and a freedom which shall not be challenged.'

'We are now free in name. The extent to which we become free in fact and secure our freedom will be the extent to which we become Gaels again.'

Michael Collins

He then turns from the minutiae of constitutional theory and practice to the more material, practical matters where he always felt on home ground.

'We got in the treaty the strongest guarantees of freedom and security that we could have got on paper … . The most realistic demonstration of the amount of real practical freedom acquired was the evacuation of the British troops and the demobilisation of the military police force. In place of the British troops, we now have our own army. In place of the RIC we are organising our own civic guard – our own people's police force.

'These things … are the plainest definition of our independence; they are the clearest recognition of our national rights … . It is the evacuation by the British which gives us our freedom. The treaty is the guarantee that that freedom shall not be violated.'

In a sense, both de Valera and Collins were right. De Valera's formula – Document No. 2 – would prove itself in time, and Collins's 'freedom to achieve freedom' was thoroughly vindicated in coming years – ironically by the manoeuvrings of the serpentine de Valera. It was de Valera who was abandoning realism on the question of the treaty, first by not himself leading the Irish delegation to London, thus depriving them of their most formidable and skilful negotiator, and second by misreading the mood of post-truce Ireland. On the immediate issue, Collins the irreconcilable hard man bent to the wind – with every degree of reluctance – and accepted the realities of power politics. De Valera, the careful pragmatist, retreated into intransigence.

The key issue was the oath of allegiance required by the treaty. For de Valera, it was an abomination, a betrayal of every republican principle. For Collins, it was a regrettable necessity, however distasteful. But the obsession with the oath meant that

North Wall, Dublin, soldiers of a British cavalry regiment prepare to leave Ireland following the signing of the Anglo-Irish Treaty.

the question of partition was almost entirely absent from the treaty debates. This reflected southern amnesia where the north was concerned, a weakness in every iteration of nationalism from O'Connell onwards. There was a comforting assumption that the new Northern Ireland statelet was too small and internally divided to survive for long. It was widely believed, and not just by nationalists, that the promised boundary commission would emasculate it to the point of non-viability. But for Collins, as we have seen and will see again below, the North remained a matter of supreme importance: over the first six months of 1922 he did everything he could to strangle it at birth.

The treaty was approved by the Dáil on a vote of 64 to 57 on 7 January 1922. De Valera resigned as president in emotional scenes and was replaced by Arthur Griffith. On 14 January, Collins was elected chairman of the Provisional Government, established under the treaty to bridge the 12 months until the final agreed departure of the British. He also retained the office of minister for finance. But it was in his role as chairman of the Provisional Government that he took possession of Dublin Castle from FitzAlan, the last British viceroy. The very heart and sinew of British power in Ireland was now securely and legally in the hands of an Irish administration. British troops began to withdraw. The police, the RIC, were gradually wound down, to be replaced by a new force. On 31 January, the new Irish army marched into Beggar's Bush barracks in Dublin – not far from de Valera's old 1916 command at Boland's Mills – and took possession of it from the British, who marched out.

British soldiers marching out of a barracks.

More than most of the republican leadership, Collins was concerned about the North. The birth of Northern Ireland under the Government of Ireland Act 1920 had unleashed an orgy of vengeful sectarian violence over the following two years. The War of Independence spread to the northern counties and became entangled with local sectarian hatreds of long standing, now compounded by the trauma – for nationalists at least – of partition. With Collins's full approval, the IRA had attacked the police and the army in Ulster. This proved counter-productive, as Protestant mobs drove Catholic workers from their places of employment, especially in the Belfast shipyards. The IRA retaliated by burning business premises and big houses in rural Ulster – all in Protestant ownership – in order to try to relieve the pressure on their beleaguered co-religionists in Belfast. The UVF was re-formed as a

People smashing and looting Belfast shops as violence erupts in the city, July 1920.

police reserve called the Ulster Special Constabulary, but better known simply as the B Specials.

In effect, the sectarian civil war that might well have broken out over Home Rule in 1914 – had the little matter of the First World War not interposed – now caught fire in the Ulster cockpit. In March 1922, with the Provisional Government establishing itself in Dublin, 61 people died in Belfast alone. Inevitably, given their local superiority in numbers and the fact that they now controlled the levers of the state, the Protestants were able to bring a greater terror to bear than the Catholics. Atrocities were committed on both sides: it was not all one-way traffic. But the Protestant traffic was more lethal.

In an attempt to help the northern nationalists, the Dáil administration had, at Collins's instigation, inaugurated a boycott of goods sourced in Belfast in August 1920. It was a futile gesture: North-South trade was not so robust as to make a boycott in any way effective. By the new year, with Collins settling down in Dublin and Sir James Craig, the new prime minister of Northern Ireland, securing his position in Belfast, it seemed time to talk rather than fight. Craig had met de Valera the previous year and had found him impossible. Now he met with Collins. He found him a lot easier to deal with and the pair reached an agreement in January 1922 in which Collins agreed to call off the Belfast Boycott in return for Craig putting a stop to the exclusion of Catholics from places of employment.

That caused a slight thaw, but it was no more than that. Collins met Craig a second time, but any attempt to suggest changes to the border met with a blank refusal in Belfast. A third and final meeting between the two men took place in London in March. It resulted in the Craig-Collins Pact in which Craig promised to recruit more Catholic police and to offer protection to Catholic shipyard workers again, while Collins promised to restrain the IRA in the North. Neither party delivered its side of the deal. Each was playing a double game. Far from giving any implicit legitimacy to the new northern statelet, Collins continued to work covertly for its subversion, by offering encouragement and support to the ongoing IRA campaign. What finally ended this insurgency in the North was not any change of heart in the South but military necessity. When civil war broke out in the Free State in June, it became expedient to deploy northern units of the IRA in support of the military situation in the South. Thus the northern revolt fizzled out.

The Cabinet of Northern Ireland in 1921. From left to right, Dawson Bates, Marquess of Londonderry; James Craig; H. M. Pollock; E. M. Archdale; J. M. Andrews.

In early 1922, the South was drifting towards civil war. An army convention in late March revealed the extent of the split. An anti-treaty IRA announced itself; on behalf of this group – soon to be known as the irregulars – Rory O'Connor repudiated the authority of the Dáil. An anti-treaty mob destroyed the machinery of the *Freeman's Journal*, a Dublin nationalist newspaper that had been continuously published since 1763. Its crime was to have been pro-treaty. In April, Rory O'Connor led a party of irregulars to occupy the Four Courts on Dublin's north quays. This led to ever-growing pressure from London on Collins to flush them out, including the threat to halt the withdrawal of British troops who would be set to do the job themselves if the Provisional Government proved unable or unwilling. Collins temporised as best he could.

In May, Collins made a pact with de Valera in respect of the forthcoming general election in which each side agreed to nominate candidates in numbers proportionate to their existing strength in the outgoing Dáil. This was a flagrant breach of one of the terms of the treaty and Collins and Griffith were summoned to London to get a dressing-down from Lloyd George, egged on by the ever belligerent Churchill, who was formally in charge of overseeing the British end of the transition of power.

Churchill had reasons for his belligerence. Not only was the Collins-de Valera pact a clear breach of the treaty, so was the continued occupation of the Four Courts by the irregulars and the failure of the Provisional Government to root them out. Then there was the assassination of Field-Marshal Sir Henry Hughes Wilson, the chief of the Imperial General Staff, military adviser to the Northern Ireland government and adamantine opponent of all Irish nationalist ambition. He was shot dead outside his house in Eaton Square in broad daylight on 22 June. It was an IRA operation, and while it could never be proved that it was done on Collins's instruction, or at least with his knowledge, Churchill was not alone in suspecting him. Things like that just did not happen without Collins being in the loop.

Field Marshall Sir Henry Hughes Wilson, British army officer.

It seems that whether from British pressure or otherwise, Collins reneged on the pact with de Valera. The general election produced 58 seats for the pro-treaty party, as against 36 for the anti-treaty candidates. The balance was made up by Labour, minor party candidates, and independents to the number of 34. Support from Labour and some of the others gave the pro-treaty faction a working majority. But by now – the second half of June – events were running away from the Dáil and towards the Four Courts, the great Georgian pile on the north bank of the Liffey that housed the Irish superior law courts.

One other factor, in addition to British pressure, influenced Collins's final decision to attack the Four Courts. This was the kidnap by the garrison there of Lt-General J. J. 'Ginger' O'Connell, the popular deputy chief of staff of the new National Army. This was a brazen challenge to the authority of the Provisional Government and to the integrity of the entire treaty settlement. It may have been the straw that broke the camel's back.

The matter was settled in the early hours of 28 June. Collins gave the go-ahead to root the irregulars out of their position. This was done using two 18-pound field guns borrowed from the British – the first use of artillery by the Irish army. Collins was now, in addition to all his other duties, about to be commander-in-chief of this army. It did the job with impressive dispatch. The Four Courts garrison, numbering about 200 men, was forced to abandon its position on 30 June, but not before one of the great tragedies of the entire Irish revolutionary saga.

The Four Courts complex was not just the headquarters of the Irish legal system. It also housed the Public Record Office (PRO), established to maintain and archive administrative and legal documents going back centuries. It had been housed originally in Dublin Castle but its holdings had been transferred to a corner of the Four Courts in 1867. It was an indispensable and irreplaceable treasure trove of historical material. On 30 June, an explosive device blew the PRO and its contents to the high heavens in an explosion heard and seen all over the city, as a dramatic plume of smoke – looking like a volcanic eruption – rose into the summer sky. Just who was responsible for this disaster – and whether it was deliberate or an accident – is still in dispute. The greater burden of suspicion lies with the irregular defendants of the Four Courts, whether through carelessness or deliberation, or some mixture of the two. But, one way or another, a lot of Irish history was reduced to ashes.

CHAPTER 11
Civil War

'Yerra, they'll
never shoot
me in my own
country.'

Michael Collins

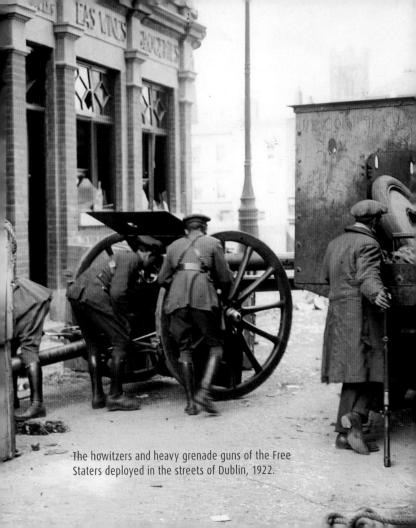

The howitzers and heavy grenade guns of the Free
Staters deployed in the streets of Dublin, 1922.

The artillery bombardment of the Four Courts began at 4 a.m. on 28 June. The irregular garrison, numbering about 200 men, was flushed out by the 30th. Meanwhile, Cathal Brugha was barricaded into the Hammam Hotel in Sackville Street (renamed O'Connell Street in 1924), on the opposite side of the street to the GPO, the side of Dublin's central thoroughfare that had suffered the least damage in 1916. Now it took its turn.

The position of the men holed up in the Hammam Hotel was hopeless. It was a reprise of the Easter Rising, the occupation of static defensive positions that were bound to yield to superior force. It was the precise opposite of every military strategy that Collins had deployed ever since the Easter Rising. Brugha had been called upon to surrender when it was obvious that his position was hopeless, but instead he charged out of the building on 5 July, all guns blazing, into the side street that now bears his name – then Gloucester Street – and was shot down. The wounds he received proved fatal. He died in the nearby Mater Hospital two days later.

Collins was moved by Brugha's death, acknowledging his raw courage, which was all of a piece with his unyielding adherence to republican absolutism. There had been no love lost between them in life, but Collins recognised a fellow warrior. With the flushing out of the irregulars in the Hammam Hotel, the Civil War in Dublin was effectively over. The Irish capital was now securely in the hands of the Provisional Government.

A war council was established on 12 July, with Collins as commander-in-chief of the National Army. By now, the war was focused on what became known as the 'Munster Republic', because anti-treaty forces were strongest in the southern province. The War of Independence had been prosecuted most tenaciously there. These facts were no coincidence.

None the less, it quickly became clear that the contest was a hopeless mismatch. As early as 20 July, the cities of Limerick

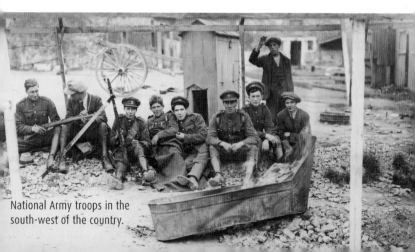

National Army troops in the south-west of the country.

and Waterford had fallen to the National Army. Cork, the provincial capital, was now the rebels' redoubt. Collins captured it with typical strategic flair and a continued belief in a war of movement. The basic strategy was elaborated by Emmet Dalton, one of Collins's closest subordinates. It involved commandeering a ship, the *Arvonia*, and sailing it down the east coast and then west towards Cork itself. The anti-treaty forces in the city were conscious that a seaborne attempt to take them was a possibility and they even mined the seaward approaches to the city. But they lacked numbers, both in men and in materiel. The landings were a success, despite the notorious difficulties attending such an operation and the utter inexperience of Dalton and the rest of them.

The southern capital fell on 10 August. The next day, anti-treaty forces evacuated Fermoy in north County Cork, their last urban possession in the province. The next day, Arthur Griffith died. He was president of Sinn Féin but not a member of the Provisional Government. Already in poor health, he was advised by his friend, the poet and surgeon Oliver St John Gogarty, to enter hospital for a few days' rest. He was admitted to St Vincent's Hospital in Dublin, while continuing to attend his office on a daily basis. Walking along a hospital corridor, he bent down to tie a loose shoelace, had a cerebral haemorrhage and died on the spot. He was 51 years old.

One of the most famous photographs we have of Michael Collins was taken at Griffith's funeral. He is dressed in full military uniform as commander-in-chief of the army, seen looking rather imperiously over his right shoulder. It was the first great state occasion for the emerging country, one in which the solemnity of funerals had always been awarded a high place in its cultural values. Few who followed Griffith's coffin that day imagined that they would be following Collins's barely a fortnight later.

What possessed Collins to go to Cork? He had no business there. The Civil War was as good as won. All that remained was a mopping-up operation, which took until the following April, when the order

Michael Collins at Arthur Griffith's funeral.

to dump arms came from the republican high command. He had hardly ventured out of Dublin during the War of Independence, so what took him south now? Well, he had already been on one tour of inspection to raise morale among National Army troops. Why not continue with another, especially as it would bring him to his native county?

It has been speculated that, with the Civil War as good as settled militarily, he hoped to persuade anti-treaty supporters in his own county to abandon what was now obviously a futile struggle. There is circumstantial and anecdotal evidence in support of this speculation, as it appears that attempts were made to arrange meetings between Collins and leading anti-treaty men like Tom Barry, all of which proved abortive. Collins felt keenly the tragic split in the army – the army that he, more than anyone, had enabled. It would have been in character for him to offer an olive branch now, especially with the military issue beyond question.

He went despite warnings from close colleagues. Joseph McGrath, a former director of intelligence and now minister for labour in the Provisional Government, thought it a mad idea. All the cities and towns had fallen to the National Army and the irregulars had retreated to the hills. But there are a lot of hills in

West Cork and it was an area with a strong presence of anti-treaty fighting men. It was all very well to sentimentalise about going back to Collins's home place; it was also the place of greatest potential danger.

None the less, he went. He stayed in the Imperial Hotel on the South Mall in Cork city, before starting out for the west of the county – his own home country – early in the morning of 22 August 1922. His escort convoy was modest, considering the risks he was running. There have been some suggestions that messages of safe conduct had reached Collins via anti-treaty back channels, but this cannot be known for certain. At any rate, the convoy comprised the following: a motor-cycle scout; an open Crossley Tender, a troop transport vehicle that had been much favoured by the British during the War of Independence, this one containing two members of Collins's Squad, eight riflemen and two machine gunners; an open touring car in which sat Michael Collins and Emmet Dalton; and an armoured car at the rear.

He first went to Macroom, an odd choice, given that his ultimate destination was Clonakilty and its environs in the south-west of the county, so a route directly through Bandon would have made more sense. It is therefore reasonable to infer that he had business of some sort to transact in Macroom, perhaps to do with peace talks. The party then swung south-east across the centre of the county to access Bandon and the road west. That took them through Béal na mBláth, a remote and beautiful valley which was an ideal ambush site. By sheer coincidence, there were a considerable number of anti-treaty republicans in the area at the time, up to and including de Valera himself, to discuss future military strategy. This group got wind of Collins's presence and, under the direction of Tom Hales, an ambush party was set up at Béal na mBláth in the hope that Collins's party would return that evening by the same route. They waited.

Meanwhile, Collins's party reached Bandon and took the road west. His presence in his home place caused the expected sensation. There was food and drink a-plenty. It will never be established if Collins or anyone else had had a lot to drink, but it is perfectly reasonable to suppose that they had all had a few – how many few we'll never know. By a great irony, one of the people he bade farewell to that day was Sean Hales TD, the senior National Army officer in the area, who would be shot dead in Dublin a few months later. At that moment, Hales's brother Tom was superintending the ambush at Béal na mBláth. The entire party turned back for Cork as evening fell, but not before Collins was warned in Rosscarbery that there was an ambush set for him at Béal na mBláth – you couldn't keep a secret for long in the Irish countryside, where rumour could spread at the speed of light. Collins shrugged it off.

This was material – and fatal – because the party chose to return as they had come, through Béal na mBláth. The obvious way back to the city was straight on at Bandon towards Innishannon and home, but instead they went back across country. It seems that Collins was expected in the village of Crookstown, a little way beyond Béal na mBláth going north. We shall never know why he was going that way; the most reasonable inference is that some sort of meeting was planned in connection with possible peace feelers.

Of course, he never made it to Crookstown. At Béal na mBláth, the ambush party had been lying in wait all day; it was now approaching 8 p.m. and the light was fading. Most of the party had given up and retired to a nearby pub. Tom Hales was busy dismantling mines and other obstacles designed to stop the convoy. Only a few of the original ambush party remained on the hillside, poorly armed, when the noise of the leading motorcycle was heard approaching, announcing the arrival of the convoy.

Once they realised what was afoot, Dalton and Collins, travelling in the open touring car, reacted in completely different ways. Dalton very sensibly shouted at the driver to 'drive like hell', obviously the correct decision. In the circumstances, the imperative was to get clear of the ambush site as fast as possible. It was Collins who overbore him, bade the driver stop and thus got involved in an ill-judged, unnecessary and fatal firefight. The details are impossible to piece together and, in a sense, don't matter. Only one person died at Béal na mBláth that evening: Michael Collins, who took a bullet to the head that left 'a fearful, gaping wound at the base of the skull and behind the right ear', in the words of Emmet Dalton, the first man to reach him. There could be no doubt about the consequence: the wound was fatal.

The whole thing had taken about 30 minutes or so. What followed was a nightmare journey back to Cork on unfamiliar roads with the body of the dead man draped over Dalton's shoulder in the armoured car. It was 1:30 a.m. before they reached Cork. The body was removed to a local hospital.

Who fired the shot that killed Michael Collins? It was for years one of the most insistent, if perhaps not the most compelling, question in modern Irish history. We know the names of the

The assassination of Michael Collins.

remaining members of the depleted ambush party; it could have been any of them. It doesn't really matter. The whole affair at Béal na mBláth was a muddle, played out in bad light and wet weather. Every man in the ambush party, from Tom Hales down, loved and admired Collins. Whichever one of them fired off the fatal shot is really neither here nor there. He was shot by a neighbour's child – one can use the term literally, for some of the ambush party were little more than children – in his own county. No one was proud of what happened. To the contrary, they were devastated, none more than Hales.

The body was brought to Dublin for burial on 28 August 1922. First, it lay in state in the City Hall before the funeral cortège made its way to the pro-Cathedral, just off Sackville Street, for the funeral Mass. Thereafter, it processed to Glasnevin Cemetery for burial in the republican plot, just inside the main gate. The crowds were immense. Hundreds of thousands lined the route. The graveside oration was given by W. T. Cosgrave, who had replaced Collins as chairman of the Provisional Government. The contrast in style could hardly have been greater. Where Collins had been charismatic, Cosgrave was decidedly not. He was anti-heroic. Yet he went on to lead the first independent Irish government for 10 years. Some of the actions he approved, especially reprisal

Michael Collins lying in state in Dublin after his murder on
22 August 1922.

killings, were to be a source of lasting bitterness and hatred, but there was enough of that already in the air because of the death of Collins. And when, in 1932, Cosgrave was voted out of office, he transferred power seamlessly to de Valera – risen from the political dead – and thus secured the integrity of Irish democracy.

Almost as insistent a question as who fired the fatal shot was what might have happened had Collins lived. It is even more futile to speculate. He had said that he wanted to focus on the army, seeing himself as a soldier rather than a politician. But, as we have seen, his formidable array of gifts, not least in administration and organisation, might have got the better of him. Besides, he had displayed a precocious political energy both in the treaty negotiations and in the Dáil debates on the treaty itself. We'll never know. As with all history, we only know what actually happened – and we know that imperfectly – and we can have no knowledge of what did not happen. What did not happen was the consequence of a freak event, an ambush at Béal na mBláth that quickly went from farce to tragedy. All else is silence.

'De mortuis nil nisi bonum': of the dead, only speak well. It is a sentiment generally honoured in the observance. What is perhaps as interesting is what people said about Collins when alive.

The interment of Michael Collins. A line of officers in the Free State Army salute. The figure in the foreground is the gravedigger.

Winston Churchill was no friend of Irish nationalist aspiration, then or afterwards – as he demonstrated more than once – but he observed Collins when, conflicted and unhappy, he had just signed the treaty in Downing Street. Churchill wrote of him, perhaps with a little pardonable exaggeration: 'Michael Collins rose looking as though he was going to shoot someone, preferably himself. In all my life, I have never seen such pain and suffering in restraint.' That gives a glimpse of the living man, and the degree of self-control, even when under extraordinary stress, that set Collins apart from others. Later, in another context, Churchill observed simply that Collins 'was an Irish patriot, true and fearless'.

After his death, George Bernard Shaw wrote a kind letter to Collins's sister Hannie as follows:

'My Dear Miss Collins –

Don't let them make you miserable about it: how could a born soldier die better than at the victorious end of a good fight, falling to the shot of another Irishman – a damned fool, but all the same an Irishman who thought he was fighting for Ireland – "A Roman to Roman"? I met Michael for the first and last time on Saturday last, and am very glad I did. I rejoice in his memory, and will not be so disloyal to it as to snivel over his valiant death. So tear up your mourning and hang up your brightest colours in his honour; and let us all praise God that he did not die in a snuffy bed of a trumpery cough, weakened by age, and saddened by the disappointments that would have attended his work had he lived.'

It is difficult to make up one's mind about this note, kindly meant though it actually was. It captured something of Collins's heroic stature, but there seems to be something too calculated and contrived about the emotions that it expresses to be completely sincere.

Playwright George Bernard Shaw.

Despite all the bitterness engendered by the Civil War – the two principal political parties of independent Ireland reflected the division – both sides retained a frank admiration for Collins. This was in sharp contrast to de Valera, who rose to a degree of popularity unprecedented since Parnell while still drawing the hatred and contempt of his opponents. Of course, de Valera lived long and made mistakes like everyone else. We may be sure that had Collins lived, he would at least have made his own mistakes. There are posthumous advantages to dying a young, heroic death. But what is remarkable is the lack of bitterness towards Collins – unlike that shown to Cosgrave – among de Valera partisans.

It was as if all could agree that what had happened was a horrible tragedy, a dishonourable accident. There was nothing to be proud of in the death of Collins. When the IRA assassinated Kevin O'Higgins in 1927, the strongman in Cosgrave's government, there was no such sentiment. Old republicans felt that O'Higgins had got no more than he deserved. You don't have to share that sentiment to mark the difference in sensibility towards the memory of Michael Collins.

Every August, on the Sunday nearest to the anniversary of his death, there is a commemoration ceremony at Béal na mBláth.

Tragically, it was for years regarded as a party event, an occasion reserved for the political successors of the pro-treaty tradition: first Cumann na nGaedheal and later its successor entity, Fine Gael. For 90 years, no member of the rival party, de Valera's Fianna Fáil, attended, let alone spoke at the commemoration. Then, in 2010, the Fianna Fáil Minister for Finance, Brian Lenihan, was invited, accepted and delivered the oration. It was an emotional occasion, the burying of a very old hatchet.

Collins is remembered – perhaps uniquely among those who made the Irish revolution and fought the Civil War – as a uniter, not a divider. He was, by any measure, a singular man.

'History will record the greatness of Michael Collins and it will be recorded at my expense.'

Éamon de Valera, 1966

Michael Collins, leader of the Irish Free State in the uniform of Commander-in-Chief of the Irish National Army.

Select Bibliography

Coogan, T.P., *Michael Collins,* Hutchinson, London 1990

Fewer, Michael, *The Battle of the Four Courts: the first three days of the Irish civil war,* Apollo, London 2018

Hopkinson, Michael, *The Irish War of Independence,* Gill & Macmillan, Dublin 2002

Hopkinson, Michael, *Green Against Green: the Irish civil war,* Gill & Macmillan, Dublin, 1988

Longford, Lord (Frank Pakenham), *Peace by Ordeal: the negotiation of the Anglo-Irish treaty 1921,* Pimlico, London 1935

Mitchell, Arthur, *Revolutionary Government in Ireland: Dáil Éireann 1919–22,* Gill & Macmillan, Dublin 1995

Ó Broin, León, ed., *In Great Haste: the letters of Michael Collins and Kitty Kiernan,* Gill & Macmillan, Dublin 1983

Townshend, Charles, *The Republic: the fight for Irish independence,* Allen Lane, London, 2013

Yeates, Pádraig, *A City in Turmoil: Dublin 1919–21,* Gill Books, Dublin 2012

Author's note

Most of the direct quotations from Collins's speeches and statements are taken from a slim volume entitled *A Path to Freedom*, attributed to Collins but with no editor or place of publication indicated. The copy that I was able to source online is sourced only to a web address: www.ezreads.net.

Picture Credits

The publisher gratefully acknowledges the following image copyright holders. All images are copyright © individual rights holders unless stated otherwise. Every effort has been made to trace copyright holders, or copyright holders not mentioned here. If there have been any errors or omissions, the publisher would be happy to rectify this in any reprint.

ABBREVIATIONS: NLI CC: National Library of Ireland Creative Commons / COL: colourised monochrome image.

p1   Wikipedia/COL
p3   Alamy
p4   De Luan/Alamy
p7   Hugh Rooney/Alamy
p9   The Granger Collection/
      Alamy
p10   Teapot Press
p11   Teapot Press
p13   Wikipedia/COL
p15   NLI CC
p17   NLI CC
p19   Vanity Fair/Teapot Press
p20   Wikipedia
p23   NLI CC
p24   Wikipedia/COL
p27   Wikipedia/COL
p29   National Archives, Public
      Record Office
p30   Steve Vidler/Alamy
p33   Wikipedia/COL
p35   National Gallery of Ireland
p37   Unknown
p38   NLI CC
p41   Wikipedia/COL
p43   Library of Congress/COL
p44   Library of Congress
p45   NLI CC
p46   Wikipedia
p47   Wikipedia
p48   Wikipedia/COL
p48   Wikipedia/COL
p49   Wikipedia/COL
p50   Pictorial Press/Alamy
p52   Library of Congress
p55   Wikipedia/COL
p56   Currier & Ives/Library of
      Congress
p57   Wikipedia/COL

p59   Wikipedia
p60   Presented, New Ireland
      Assurance Company, 2016/
      National Gallery of Ireland
p60   Wikipedia
p62   Pictorial Press Ltd/Alamy
p65   Kate Loz/Teapot Press
p66   Wikipedia
p67   History & Art Collection/
      Alamy
p68   Unknown
p71   National Gallery of Ireland
p72   Kate Loz/Teapot Press
p74   World History Archive/Alamy
p76   De Luan/Alamy
p77   Historical Images Archive/
      Alamy
p78   De Luan/Alamy
p80   Kate Loz/Teapot Press
p81   Granger Historical Picture
      Archive/Alamy
p83   Unknown
p85   DRI Creative Commons
p87   Mick O'Dea
p88   Courtesy of the Irish
      Capuchin Archives
p90   Teapot Press
p91   Pictorial Press Ltd/Alamy
p93   Wikipedia/COL
p95   NLI CC/COL
p97   Wikipedia
p98   Wikipedia
p99   John J. Burns Library, Boston
      College
p99   John J. Burns Library, Boston
      College
p100 Pictorial Press Ltd/Alamy
p103 RTÉ Archives

p104 Wikipedia
p107 Unknown
p108 Wikipedia/family album
p110 Wikipedia/COL
p111 Wikipedia/COL
p113 Courtesy of the Irish
      Capuchin Archives
p115 Granger Historical Picture
      Archive/Alamy
p119 Seamus Culligan/Alamy
p120 NLI CC
p124 Wikipedia
p125 Courtesy of the Irish
      Capuchin Archives/
      COL Teapot Press
p126 Vanity Fair/Teapot Press
p127 Wikipedia/unknown
p128 DRI Creative Commons
p130 Wikipedia/COL
p131 Wikipedia
p132 Unknown/enhanced
p135 Pictorial Press Ltd/Alamy
p137 Courtesy of the Irish
      Capuchin Archives/
      COL Teapot Press
p139 Unknown
p141 NLI CC
p145 Courtesy of the Irish
      Capuchin Archives
p146 Library of Congress/COL
p149 Wikipedia
p155 NLI CC
p157 NLI CC
p159 Library of Congress
p160 Bhanu Prakash Kushwaha/
      Teapot Press
p163 NLI CC/COL
p164 Cork City/COL

p167 NLI CC
p169 South Dublin Library
p171 Bhanu Prakash Kushwaha/
      Teapot Press
p171 Unknown/Enhanced
p172 Bhanu Prakash Kushwaha/
p174 Teapot Press
p181 Courtesy of the Irish
      Capuchin Archives
p182 Wikipedia
      Library of Congress/COL
p187 De Luan/Alamy
p189 Unknown
p191 Bhanu Prakash Kushwaha/
      Teapot Press
p192 Wikipedia/COL
p195 NLI CC/COL
p197 De Luan/Alamy
p199 Wikipedia/COL
p202 NLI CC
p211 De Luan/Alamy
p213 PA Images/Alamy
p215 Wikipedia
p216 NLI CC
p222 NLI CC
p225 NLI CC
p226 Illustrated London News/
      Teapot Press
p229 Illustrated London News/CO
p231 Chronicle/Alamy
p235 Agefotstock/Alamy
p237 NLI CC
p239 Pictorial Press Ltd/Alamy
p245 Chronicle/Alamy
p247 Pictorial Press Ltd/Alamy
p248 NLI CC
p251 Project Gutenberg/Wikiped
p254 Alburn/Alamy